AUTHENTICITY

Also by David Posen, MD

Is Work Killing You?
The Little Book of Stress Relief
Staying Afloat When the Water Gets Rough
Always Change a Losing Game

AUTHENTICITY

A GUIDE TO LIVING IN HARMONY WITH YOUR TRUE SELF

David Posen, MD

AMBROSIA

Published in Canada in 2018 and the USA in 2018
by House of Anansi Press Inc.
www.houseofanansi.com

House of Anansi Press is committed to protecting our natural environment. As
part of our efforts, the interior of this book is printed on paper that contains 100%
post-consumer recycled fibres, is acid-free, and is processed chlorine-free.

22 21 20 19 18   1 2 3 4 5

Library and Archives Canada Cataloguing in Publication

Posen, David B., author
Authenticity : a guide to living in harmony with your true
self / David Posen, MD.

Issued in print and electronic formats.
ISBN 978-1-4870-0277-0 (softcover).—ISBN 978-1-4870-0278-7 (EPUB).—
ISBN 978-1-4870-0279-4 (Kindle)

1. Self-realization. 2. Self-consciousness (Awareness). I. Title.

BF637.S4P67 2018   158.1   C2016-907274-6
                    C2016-907275-4

Library of Congress Control Number: 2016958343

Book design: Alysia Shewchuk

Illustration credits: p. 17 "Personality and Optimal Arousal," copyright © Brian Little;
p. 127 "Factors Affecting Sleep," adapted from the work of William Dement.

Canada Council   Conseil des Arts
for the Arts   du Canada

ONTARIO ARTS COUNCIL
CONSEIL DES ARTS DE L'ONTARIO
an Ontario government agency
un organisme du gouvernement de l'Ontario

*We acknowledge for their financial support of our publishing program
the Canada Council for the Arts, the Ontario Arts Council, and the Government of
Canada through the Canada Book Fund.*

Printed and bound in Canada

To the late Clare McKeon, my editor, mentor, and friend, who championed this book from the very outset but tragically never got to finish it with me.

This above all: to thine own self be true,
And it must follow, as the night the day,
Thou canst not then be false to any man.
—William Shakespeare

Be yourself; everyone else is already taken.
—Oscar Wilde

CONTENTS

SECTION 3
THE SLEEP YOU NEED VS. THE SLEEP YOU GET

SECTION 4
THE VALUES YOU ESPOUSE VS. THE VALUES YOU LIVE

SECTION 5
LIVING YOUR PASSIONS VS. FOLLOWING OTHER PATHS

ROUND PEGS IN SQUARE HOLES — THE STRESS OF TRYING TO BE WHAT YOU'RE NOT

Kimberly was a shy, quiet eight-year-old girl, not unlike her father. Her mother in contrast was bubbly and gregarious and kept urging her to be more outgoing. She tried to fake it but remembers feeling ill at ease, uncomfortable, trying to be the little girl her mother wanted her to be. Faking it was taking a toll. Kimberly developed headaches that lasted for years without her realizing why. Only in her twenties did she begin to understand what was happening. "I started to pay attention to my own feelings," she said, "identifying them, acknowledging them, and accepting them." Shortly thereafter, her symptoms resolved.

How many people find themselves in situations where they're uncomfortable and don't know why? They feel like something's off or not quite right. Then they might start to feel inadequate. Even worse, they may blame themselves and feel guilty. Or they sense what the problem is but keep trying to be what others — especially parents, siblings, teachers, friends, and eventually bosses and spouses — want or expect them to be. Instead of honouring their feelings, they do what they feel is necessary to fit in. But always at a cost.

I'm a pretty fast skier — but not as fast as my older brothers. For years I tried to keep up with them, but it was more stressful than fun. Finally, I got some sense, gave up, and just skied at my own pace and met them at the bottom of the hill. When I accepted my own rhythm, my own comfortable speed—still pretty fast—it was exhilarating and I loved it.

A friend of mine came from a family of lawyers. He was expected to follow in their footsteps. He reluctantly complied and went to law school—which he roundly disliked. Finally, he decided to do what *he* wanted to do. He left law school, went to teachers' college and began a teaching career—which he soundly *enjoyed*.

Journalist Arianna Huffington tells the story of being sleep deprived for years because there were so many important things she wanted to do in her career in addition to being a mother. Sleep wasn't high on the list. It finally caught up with her when she collapsed in her office, hit her head on the desk, and broke her cheekbone. That was the wake-up moment for her when she realized the importance of slumber. She started getting the sleep she needed and became a whole new person. Now a passionate advocate, she started what she calls the "Sleep Revolution."

One of my patients worked in the accounting department of a company. When he was told to fiddle with the numbers in order to make them look better, he felt uncomfortable and lost a few nights of sleep, tossing and turning, wondering what to do. He finally decided that he couldn't live with himself if he went along with the plan. So he quit his well-paying job because the values conflict he experienced wasn't worth it to him.

> "I've always expected myself to be a really good baseball player. I feel at times I chased the numbers. I wanted to be the power guy...I was searching, trying to be somebody I wasn't and I feel like... I've gotten back to the guy that I always was, just competing and trying to be a good baseball player on both sides of the ball."
> —Justin Smoak, 2017 American League All-Star First Baseman

These examples reflect problems that patients have brought to me for more than thirty years of stress counselling. There's a recurring pattern. As life has gotten faster, fragmented, and frenetic, a lot of folks have become disconnected from who they really are. They're like round pegs trying to squeeze into square holes. Much of the anxiety and depression that people suffer is a result of this conflict of trying to be what they're not designed or inclined to be. They're living lives that feel inauthentic.

This book is about the stress that comes from trying to be what you're not—and about how to live more in harmony with yourself. It's about being more self-aware and recognizing these (sometimes subtle) areas of conflict. Encompassing the insights of physiology, psychology, and philosophy, the book will explore five seemingly unrelated realms in which *knowing* yourself better will allow you to make more informed and realistic choices in life.

If you live in ways that are authentic, congruent, and true to yourself, you can live in sync with who you really are.

SECTION 1

INTROVERSION
VS.
EXTRAVERSION

CHAPTER 1

INTROVERTS AND EXTRAVERTS

My friend Peter is a real presence. He's a big guy in every way. First of all, he's 6'4" and weighs 235 pounds. He has a deep resonant voice, a hearty laugh, and an enthusiastic personality. He's outgoing, funny, and gregarious, and anyone who ever saw him do musical comedy on stage still talks about his brilliant performances. I'd known Peter for over thirty years when he shocked me with a piece of information that I never knew or suspected. Here's how it happened.

Peter called one night to say that he was coming to town to conduct a seminar at the University of Toronto.

I said, "That's great! Can we have dinner after?"

"I'm counting on it."

"When do you finish?"

"Five o'clock."

"OK. How about we pick you up at the school around five thirty?"

"Actually, it would be better if you picked me up at my hotel at seven."

"Why? We'll lose half the evening that way."

That's when he laid it on me. "I'm an introvert and I need an hour or two to recover after a full-day workshop." I was stunned! You could have knocked me over with a feather. This guy could command a room just by walking through the door. People loved being around him. *If he's an introvert*, I thought, *then I must be Rip Van Winkle*. I couldn't fathom what he was saying.

When I finally asked what he was talking about, Peter explained, "Introversion isn't about whether or not you're outgoing. It's about how you get your energy. Teaching all day drains me. I need downtime to get my energy back."

Thus began my education about introverts and extraverts: how they differ and what the significance is for each person and the people they interact with. This isn't just interesting information. It has huge implications for how we manage our lives and how we understand and get along with others.

Then I thought about my own experiences as a presenter of lectures and seminars. I'm an extravert in terms of outgoing behaviour. But I'm also an extravert in the sense that after a speech or workshop, especially if it's been lively and fun, I feel totally energized. I'm fully alert driving home and can feel "up" for hours after.

Which Side Are *You* On?

Susan Cain is a former Wall Street lawyer who left the high-powered legal world to start her own consulting firm. She then went on to write a landmark book about introversion, *Quiet: The Power of Introverts in a World That Can't Stop Talking*. Extensively researched and beautifully written, *Quiet* was a megabestseller and has since become a classic. In her introduction, Cain uses a self-assessment tool posing twenty questions that readers can answer true or false. It's not a rating-scale exercise, but it helps people see where they stand on the introvert-extravert spectrum.

Here are some examples of introverting tendencies:

- I prefer one-on-one conversations to group activities.

- I enjoy solitude.

- I dislike small talk, but I enjoy talking in depth about topics that matter to me.

- People tell me that I'm a good listener.

- I tend to think before I speak.

- I feel drained after being out and about, even if I've enjoyed myself.

Lesley Sword of Gifted & Creative Services Australia developed an Introversion-Extraversion Indicator that lists twenty-five characteristics of extraverts. Here is a sample:

- I like to interact with many people.

- I dislike time alone.

- I prefer variety in conversation to depth.

- In a new situation, I prefer to talk rather than listen.

- I often think out loud.

- I get energy by being with people.

There are two important caveats to any self-rating scales and the scores that result. First, most tests are subjective, not scientifically objective and precise. The second is that the terms "introvert" and "extravert" are inclinations or predispositions that exist on a spectrum, not a strict dichotomy where you're clearly either one or the other. We all fall somewhere on the continuum between introversion and extraversion. It's helpful to think in terms of preferences or tendencies rather than absolute labels where you're on one extreme end or the other.

Most of us have a mix of both introvert and extravert traits. Statistically, 25 to 30 percent of the population are introverts, and 70 to 75 percent are extraverts. However, according to the Meyers-Briggs Type Indicator, the ratio in America is 50:50. There appears to be no gender difference in these groups.

Introverts Can Be Outgoing

One of the eye-opening lessons I learned from my friend Peter was that introverts aren't necessarily quiet, retiring types. They are often lively and gregarious. Here's a story that brought this home to me in a major way: I spent the week of my fiftieth birthday in Minneapolis with my twin sister and her family. We went out one night to a karaoke bar—a first for me—and it was a lot of fun. There were about a dozen in our group, but one woman particularly really got into it. She was animated and demonstrative and had a great singing voice. She seemed like a cross between Shirley MacLaine and Liza Minnelli in their primes or Beyoncé and Lady Gaga today. She brought the house down with her rendition of "These Boots Are Made for Walkin'." Whenever there was a lull, the emcee would call on her to do another song. She was terrific. We loved it.

Her performance, though, was a real shock to all of us. We'd known this woman for a long time as a soft-spoken, sweet, some-what reserved, albeit warm and friendly, individual. What we saw that night was a totally different person. It was like she'd gone into a phone booth as Clark Kent and come out as Superman (or, in this case, Wonder Woman). She was dancing and prancing and singing up a storm like the best stage performers in Vegas. But I was the most stunned of all. After all, I'd been married to this woman for *ten years*! I'd just never seen that side of her before.

Most introverts are actually quite sociable and engaging, and they enjoy other people's company. Like extraverts, they get a boost in mood from interaction with other people. But only for so long. There's a limit to their tolerance for long periods of socializing.

NOTE: Introversion and extraversion are two aspects of what we call "temperament," which is a collection of inherited traits. Among the many aspects of temperament are characteristics such as activity and energy level, adaptability, mood, distractibility, persistence, and sensitivity. I'm choosing to focus on only one area of temperament relating to introversion and extraversion because of the impact this information has had on my patients. Self-awareness in this area has helped them understand themselves better (often for the first time) and then to live their lives differently based on these insights. In many cases it's been profoundly eye-opening and even liberating.

CHAPTER 2

BACKGROUND HISTORY AND PHYSIOLOGY

Dr. Brian Little is a brilliant, engaging, funny, and award-winning psychology professor, previously at Carleton University in Ottawa and Harvard, and most recently at Cambridge.

I first heard Dr. Little on a radio interview in the 1980s and was riveted by what he had to say. I wrote away for his article "Personality Myths about Leaders," in which he discussed a fascinating premise. He explained that introverts and extraverts have different levels of activity and arousal in the cerebral cortex of the brain. Who do you think has more? You might surmise that extraverts—with their outgoing, energetic personalities—would have more cortical activity, and that introverts—who often seem quieter, even shy—would have less. Here's the surprise: it's the other way around. Paradoxically, introverts have *more* electrical activity than extraverts. That explains a lot in terms of behaviour but also in terms of stress.

A patient of mine was describing her shifts in mood and energy during and after busy social activities. She could be the life of the party, chatting and schmoozing

> You might expect that lively, noisy extraverts have more electrical activity in their brains than quiet, reserved introverts. Paradoxically, it's the other way around.

with the best of them. But then she'd get tired, a little irritable and a bit flat. I thought of Dr. Little's article, so I asked if she was an introvert or an extravert. She said, "Oh, I'm an extravert!" Suspecting the opposite, I ran the science by her and suggested that she might actually be an introvert. The very notion shocked her. It seemed totally incongruous. A lot of her professional and community activities involved social gatherings, networking, and glad-handing (she was involved in politics) — and she was really good at it.

But then she had one of those lightbulb moments. "This is amazing. I mean, I can work a room as well as anyone! But it exhausts me. This explains so much!" This simple piece of information clarified experiences that she'd never understood before. For example, she sometimes declined social invitations even though she thought of herself as a real "people person." She was now able to let go of the guilt she felt when she opted to be alone. She also understood her confusion when she'd be enjoying a social situation and suddenly feel herself shutting down and wanting to go home and be quiet. That was a pivotal moment for her — both in self-awareness and in learning to pace herself better. More awareness leads to better choices.

This illustrates an interesting dynamic. We all have a public face and a private inner person. How we present ourselves to the world is a function of our individual personality and the social situations we find ourselves in. Some people are so good at acting their public face that they can actually fool themselves into believing that they are extraverts when, temperamentally, the opposite might be true.

Swiss psychiatrist Carl Jung introduced the concept of introversion and extraversion in terms of energy expenditure and recovery in 1921. He classified personality types into the categories of "introvert" and "extravert" according to the individual's attitude to the external world. The word "extravert," coined by

Jung, was formed from the Latin words *"extra,"* meaning "out-side," and *"vertere,"* meaning "to turn." Jung formed the word "introvert" from the Latin *"intro,"* meaning "inward."

Jung developed a personality typology that became very pop-ular. He described introverts as people who prefer their inter-nal world of thoughts, feelings, and reflection, and extraverts as people who prefer the external world of things, people, and activities. (Jung probably had more time for introspection and thinking about these things because he considered himself to be an introvert—and introverts are more prone to reflection and contemplation than busy extraverts.)

The words have since become confused with ideas like shy-ness and sociability, but Jung intended them to refer to whether you more often face toward outer reality or inner reality.

Biological Differences

We're now aware that the different tendencies of behaviour and focus actually have a biological basis. And these differences can be seen early. In his acclaimed book, *Me, Myself, and Us: The Science of Personality and the Art of Well-being*, Dr. Brian Little combines cutting-edge research with his trademark humour to discuss personality traits with a lot of attention to introversion. One piece of information caught my eye in particular.

Guess how early our tendencies toward introversion or extra-version can be observed. Would you believe *in the newborn nurs-ery?* "Such features of personality can be detected in the neonatal ward. If you make a loud noise near the newborns, what will they do? Some will orient toward the noise, and others will turn away. Those who are attracted to the noise end up being extraverts later in development; those who turn away are more likely to end up being introverts."

There is another difference between introverts and extraverts: their preference for stimulation. Hans Eysenck was an eminent psychologist who was born in Germany but spent his professional life in England. He hypothesized that people seek "just right" levels of stimulation, neither too much nor too little. Eysenck believed that extraverts prefer more stimulation than introverts.

Introverts and extraverts are wired differently. Knowing the biological differences clarifies so much and is a useful foundation for understanding what happens in the real world with these two types of people. Once you appreciate that extra- and introverting tendencies are actually related to how much stimulation you prefer, you can start to choose what kind of situations you want to be in.

> "Why do extraverts have voice mail? To never miss a call. Why do introverts have voice mail? To never answer the phone." — Devora Zack

To review, it all has to do with the level of electrical activity in the part of the brain called the neocortex. Levels of neocortical arousal are different in introverts and extraverts — and are the opposite of what you'd expect. Introverts are chronically overstimulated (they rev too fast, so to speak). Extraverts are chronically understimulated (revving too slow, as it were).

This simple piece of information has helped my patients — and me — to understand much that follows from it. It has led to many flashes of insight and self-awareness, clarifying not only our own inner experiences but our understanding of other people as well. This information has great relevance for individual tendencies and abilities, social interaction styles, motivation, academic and work performance, and much more.

Let's see how it works. For the neocortex to function properly, it needs to be activated to an optimum level, referred to as an optimal level of arousal or OLA (I'm not a big fan of acronyms, but this one is less of a mouthful!). Feeling dozy is a function of low cortical arousal; feeling hyped up or overstimulated reflects a too-high level of cortical arousal.

Extraverts are chronically under the OLA needed to perform their tasks. They need more cortical arousal to get them up to full function. So they seek out stimulation from their environment to get to a level where work and other activities can be done effectively. They want things to be busier, lights brighter, sounds louder. They want more action. They tend to drive faster and move more.

By contrast, introverts are already overstimulated. They're chronically *over* the OLA. As a result, they seek respite from overload and too much stimulation, preferring quieter settings. They often retreat to be by themselves and may appear unsociable. In fact, they're just trying to calm their brain activity and recover themselves.

Just to throw in a little wrinkle here, there's a third group called "ambiverts" (similar to people who are ambidextrous). These folks are at the OLA so can go either way, depending on the situation. That is, they can act in an extraverted or introverted way. Dr. Little uses an elegantly simple diagram to illustrate the point.

Personality and Optimal Arousal

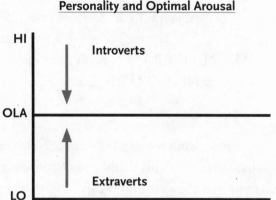

Now let's look at how all this theory plays out in our day-to-day lives.

CHAPTER 3

IMPLICATIONS AND CONSEQUENCES

All of this theory is very interesting, but what are the real-world effects of these different tendencies and styles? The short answer is, they are many and they are significant. They're important for understanding and managing ourselves and living more authentic and congruent lives. They're especially valuable in managing our stress levels because introverts and extraverts have different tolerance to stress: the fight-or-flight response can push an introvert's level of arousal even higher. Lastly, they help us to understand and thus get along better with other people.

Social Interaction Style

I had another teacher who taught me a lot about introverts: my wife, Susan. It took me a long time to understand the other side of my personable, engaging, and very funny girlfriend turned fiancée and then spouse. Susan finds excessive socializing to be tiring. She likes quiet time. She doesn't like small talk. She prefers one-on-one or small-group conversations, and finds large parties a chore (and often a bore!). She's a very good listener. She likes people to ask her questions rather than having to start conversations and talk about herself. And she finds my talkative nature a bit wearing at times.

Susan also taught me a valuable lesson about myself. One day she said, "I think sometimes you talk as much as you do to keep yourself awake." Ouch! *That* took a moment to register. At first I was defensive about this somewhat negative observation. But then I thought, *what an amazing insight.* It was also a moment of truth for me. I've learned to listen attentively to my patients, but, after a while, I need to interject or participate to keep from losing my focus. The research on extraverts totally confirmed her impression.

Dr. Little notes that conflict can arise between introverts and extraverts if they are in a closed system where trade-offs are required. An example is how many lights are on in the house. My wife prefers soft lighting. I'm up for "the brighter the better." So we go through this dance where I turn lights on and she turns them off. I turn them up; she turns them down. We say good night to dinner guests with the front hall lights low. Susan likes the mellow mood it creates. I feel I can hardly see the people, much less find their coats in the closet. I'll often find her reading in the family room with one low light on. It looks like she's reading in the dark. But to her, it's the perfect setting.

Introverts enjoy solitude and feel drained after too much social interaction. Extraverts enjoy excitement, lots of activity, socializing—and feel de-energized by too much solitude. Marti Olsen Laney is an authority on introversion and the introverted author of the excellent books *The Introvert Advantage* and *The Introvert and Extrovert in Love.* In the latter, she relates a telling story involving her extraverted husband, Michael, who was her co-author. Mike is a consultant who works with many businesses and companies, including media giants like the Walt Disney Company and Warner Brothers. He had planned a large cowboy-themed party at the Warner Brothers back lot in Burbank. It was starting while she was preparing to curl up in bed with a good book. Mike called her at 9 p.m. and again at 10, urging her to come over. "It's a great party," he said. He couldn't imagine why she'd pass up such a fun experience. It never occurred to him that she was *already* having a good time, alone at home.

When we first got married, I'd wake up in the morning and start chatting with Susan. To my surprise, she didn't seem to enjoy that much. Nor did she join in. Finally, she informed me that she liked quiet in the morning until she "got going." I'd grown up with extraverted siblings — we all chattered away when we got up. Now I understand the physiology behind her reaction. Good lesson too — both our sons are like their mom, so my early learning about their preferences for morning quiet has stood me in good stead.

Another interesting area of difference relates to nonverbal communication. Jerry Seinfeld and Larry David are master observers of the subtleties of human behaviour. They did a whole *Seinfeld* episode on "close talkers" with Judge Reinhold playing a guy who got really in your face when talking to people. We all have our own comfort zone for interacting with people. It's like an invisible bubble around us. We feel uncomfortable when others get too close and we feel disconnected if they're too far away. In general, extraverts tend to stand closer, establish a lot of eye contact, engage in extensive (often unsolicited) body contact (such as touching, putting a hand on someone's shoulder), and behave in ways that increase their overall level of stimulation. In social settings, they tend to be happy, outgoing, warm, and curious. Introverts, by contrast, tend to stand farther apart, avert their gaze, avoid unnecessary contact, and modulate their interactive exchanges. Here's an even finer distinction: introverts make good eye contact when listening but less when speaking. Extraverts have good eye contact when speaking but less when listening.

These differences reflect the physiological basis of extraversion and introversion. But there's a cultural overlay as well. Some cultures place a high premium on extraverted conduct (for example, North America and many Middle Eastern countries, where people are more animated), while others place a high premium on introverted conduct (for example, Finland, England, and Japan, where people tend to be more reserved.) This can lead to what anthropologist Ned Hall playfully calls the "United Nations Dance," where both groups are attempting to be polite. This can be appreciated when these groups are filmed interacting: one person quietly advances while the other subtly retreats.

Silence is another issue that can present problems and misunderstanding. Introverts need time to think, process what's going on, and formulate ideas. Extraverts talk a lot and are uncomfortable with silences. They get impatient waiting for a response. Or they misconstrue the meaning of the silence, interpreting it as rudeness, purposeful withholding, or even incompetence.

Here's a scenario I've watched many times in my office. In couple counselling, there's often a verbal spouse and a quiet spouse. The extravert might make a comment or ask a question and, when the introvert doesn't respond right away, the extravert starts talking again—either rewording the question or repeating the point they were making. I watch the introvert start to tune out. Not only is the extravert interrupting their thought process, but the introvert also feels overloaded by the combination of their own internal dialogue and the droning on of their loquacious partner. It's like an inner form of mental multitasking—which is both stressful and frustrating. I sometimes intervene and ask the extravert to stop talking. "Hold on a sec. Give them time to answer. They're processing what you just said." I can almost see the wheels thoughtfully turning in the introvert's brain, but the chatty spouse is talking over them because they assume silence means a lack of attention, engagement, or effort. Introverts are comfortable with silence. Extraverts are not.

In relationships, introverts might be delayed reactors. If something bothers them, they won't always say so at the time. The other person might sense that something is wrong but have to guess for a while what it might be. The introverts need to think about what has happened and then decide how they want to handle it or present it to the other person. This can be frustrating or confusing to others, but usually the issue will eventually be addressed.

Speaking Style

In general, introverts have softer voices, appear calm, pause often, and may sound hesitant. Extraverts speak loudly, show facial expressions, move their body, interrupt others, and tend to sound authoritative. Introverts like to be asked questions. They don't volunteer information readily. Extraverts talk spontaneously. Introverts think before they act or speak. Extraverts may speak without thinking. Someone called this "shooting from the hip—and the lip!"

In group discussions extraverts usually do most of the talking while introverts do most of the listening. Brainstorming sessions to solve a problem or generate new ideas are more suited to extraverts and don't work as well for introverts. The latter prefer time to think about things before throwing ideas out on the table. And they're often afraid of being judged—so they may shut down if they put out an idea (usually well considered before it's spoken) and someone mocks or dismisses it. They'd rather share their ideas after the meeting, perhaps by email. Also, in giving a presentation or introducing a guest speaker, extraverts are comfortable speaking extemporaneously. Introverts prefer a prepared text, even if they have to memorize it or practise it in advance.

Extraverts like to think out loud. Someone famously said: "I don't know what I'm thinking till I hear what I have to say!" That person was undoubtedly an extravert. Extraverts like to solve problems verbally — using others as a sounding board. I've had many patients do this. They do most of the talking and work out solutions themselves, while I just ask a few questions and provide a safe space and attentive ear. As an extravert, I have often found it helpful to talk through issues. Years ago I hired a consultant to help me redesign one of my seminars. He gave me a lot of good ideas and suggestions. But often he just provoked my thinking and then listened while I talked myself into or out of certain options. Introverts, on the other hand, like to think things through internally to make decisions.

This raises an important point about all these differences. Just knowing this information can be very comforting and even validating in understanding ourselves better. But it also increases our awareness about how *other* people function and helps us appreciate characteristics about them that may have mystified us. After the first lecture I ever gave on this subject, a man came up to me and said, enthusiastically, "Thank you so much for this. I only wish I'd heard it thirty years ago. Now I finally understand my wife!"

Learning and the Way We Learn

Who does better in school? It appears that introverts do, some-times *a lot* better. Extraverts need more hands-on, active kinds of learning—asking questions, learning by doing—whereas introverts need structure and order. Their learning is deeper and more reflective. Introverts learn best in quiet conditions, and extraverts do better with more noise. This makes perfect sense given the differences in brain wiring. Noise increases the optimal level of arousal of extraverts but pushes introverts over the top of their OLA.

This speaks to a big problem in the way current school class-rooms are organized. When I was in grade school we sat in rows. Today, the desks are configured in clusters (or pods) to enhance group work and learning. This presents the same kind of prob-lem as open concept offices in the workplace. They're great for extraverts but not for introverts, who prefer solitude and work-ing independently. Introverts need peace and quiet in order to concentrate—and to perform well both at school and at work.

Memory

Differences in learning style may help to explain why introverts do better academically than extraverts, but memory also plays a part. It turns out that there's a difference here as well. Memory is organized differently in extraverts and introverts. Extraverts have better short-term memory and do better on short-term memory tasks. Introverts have better long-term memory and do better on long-term memory tasks.

Extraverts put more of what they hear into short-term

memory. As a result, they tend to be good "on their feet" and can often create the illusion of competence by relying on short-term skills. Extraverts are often able to cram for speeches, exams, or briefings that would be disastrous for introverts. This information really resonated for me. It explained episodes in high school when my mind wandered and suddenly the teacher asked me a question. I was able to wing it; by quickly pulling together the previous few minutes of discussion, I could come up with a credible answer. I can remember occasions when I was chairing a meeting and had left the preparation until the last moment — a very extraverting trait (procrastinators, take note!). I'd hurriedly scan my notes, put together an agenda minutes before entering the room, and then fly by the seat of my pants, somehow appearing organized and well prepared. Fortunately, I don't do this anymore!

Work Style and Performance

We all seek an optimal level of arousal to function at our best. Too little or too much impairs our performance. As noted in the section on learning styles, open concept offices (which have become all the rage in recent years) create the wrong environment for introverts to do their best work. Aside from the lack of privacy, the constant noise and distraction are counterproductive to concentration and innovation. Susan Cain notes that open concept offices reduce productivity and impair memory. They're associated with high staff turnover and can make people sick, hostile, unmotivated, and insecure. They also induce many symptoms of stress and actually raise cortisol levels. I'm an extravert, but, even for me, the idea of doing high concentration work (writing this book, for example) would be unthinkable—or at least much more difficult—in an open concept office.

Extraverts tend to be procrastinators. Big time! They are likely to delay preparing or doing tasks until close to the deadline. The pressure increases their arousal and performance. It's called "the scalloping effect." This was the way I operated in the early years of my speaking career. I'd be writing up my program in a hotel room late into the evening the night before, or at the breakfast table on the morning of my presentation. There was a lot of stress and sweating—and even occasional panic—in those days.

Contrast this tale to one about my wife, a card-carrying introvert. At about the same time as I was doing my last-minute high-wire acts, Susan was the host of a local public affairs television show. Her weekly hour-long program featured an interview with a guest followed by a phone-in. She was very good at it: poised, articulate, warm, and engaging—a great television presence. But she was also exceedingly well prepared. I'd find her working on her shows two or three weeks in advance, carefully doing her research and mapping out questions. Days before, she'd be rehearsing her introduction and memorizing key parts of the interview. On screen, she was a natural, appearing relaxed and comfortable. I marvelled at Susan's discipline and proactive planning. Introverts start early on things (a project, a report, a presentation) to avoid last-minute pressure and stress. On the other hand, Susan would say to me, "I don't know how you can leave things to the last minute. I would find the stress unbearable!"

Having learned from my wife and from my own last-minute dramatics, I've become more introverting in this aspect of my work style. I now prepare well in advance and the resultant feeling of calm is both palpable and profound.

Reactions to Drugs

Believe it or not, introverts and extraverts even react differently to drugs and chemicals. When you think back to the basic difference in the inherent level of brain arousal and activity, this makes perfect sense.

Let's start with one of society's favourite drugs — alcohol. Ethyl alcohol is a cortical sedative drug. It's a central nervous system depressant. As such, it can quiet the overactivity in the brain of introverts, enhancing their performance in social situations. Introverts often feel more relaxed in social settings with a bit of alcohol as a "social lubricant." It removes inhibitions and lowers arousal levels. The wife of one of my introverted patients told me that he was much more outgoing, gregarious, and funny at parties when he'd had a few beers. Mind you, a few more drinks after that and he started slurring his words, behaving badly, and embarrassing the heck out of her.

> "It's easier to sedate an extravert than an introvert."
> — Dr. Brian Little

As an extravert, I find that alcohol just makes me sleepy. We used to go to the theatre with another couple in which the husband was also an extravert. We'd have dinner first, including a couple of glasses of wine. Unbeknownst to either of us, our wives used to bet on which of the guys would be the first to fall asleep. I now refrain from alcohol before attending a concert or play.

> The alcohol content of one beer, one five-ounce glass of wine, or one and a half ounces of liquor is roughly the same. Generally speaking, moderate drinking is considered one or two drinks a day — and preferably not *every* day.

How about caffeine? Is there any difference there? You bet. Caffeine is a cortical stimulant. It helps extraverts perform more effectively but causes problems for introverts, worsening their performance. One of the few times I purposely drink caffeine is when I have to drive long distances, especially late in the day. It keeps me alert at the wheel. My wife, on the other hand, would be wired for the day if she had even one cup of coffee in the morning.

Here's a fascinating story to illustrate the effects of caffeine. A patient, Margaret, had three startling revelations related to coffee. The first two happened at home, the third in my office. When I asked her to go off caffeine for three weeks, she wasn't pleased. (I do this experiment with all my patients so they can discover for themselves the effect this stimulant is having on them.) I told her, "I get more bang for my buck from this one recommendation than almost anything else I suggest to patients." She reluctantly agreed to do the experiment. (Warning: this *must* be done *gradually* to avoid withdrawal headaches, which are true migraines and they're brutal.) I also asked her to go to bed earlier because she wasn't getting enough sleep.

Margaret came back two weeks later and announced, "Giving up caffeine made a huge difference. I can't believe it. It's amazing! I *so* wanted you to be wrong, but you made a believer out of me." She was feeling more calm and relaxed, was sleeping better and waking up totally different, refreshed, and ready to go. "I bounce out of bed."

The second "aha" moment started with an innocent mistake. Margaret dropped into a coffee shop for a decaf and ordered something called an americano, not realizing it was caffeinated. That one drink, after being off caffeine for a few weeks, really hit her. She felt jittery, slept poorly, and her energy took a nosedive. She said, "I lost *two days*. That slipup was a great lesson!"

The third revelation came at her next appointment. Upon hearing about the profound effects of just that one coffee, I suspected that she was an introvert. When I asked her, she wasn't sure—until I explained the term in reference to how she got her energy. She immediately replied, "Based on that, I'm an introvert—*big time!* Withdrawing and cocooning is what I need—*a lot*—every day. That's where I get my energy. But I can also be very outgoing, the life of the party."

The main sources of caffeine are coffee, tea, cola drinks, and chocolate. Add to the list some over-the-counter pain medications and energy drinks such as Red Bull, Monster, and Rockstar.

This was a moment of self-discovery I have witnessed countless times in my office. Margaret gave a perfect description of an introvert although she'd never thought of herself that way until that moment. And it all came to light because of her inadvertent slip with caffeine and the impact it had on her. Again, when she became more aware, she began making better choices.

CHAPTER 4

MOTIVATIONAL DIFFERENCES

If we keep in mind the differences in inherent levels of arousal in the brain, differences in motivational styles also start to make sense and are even predictable. Introverts are uncomfortable with conflict and will avoid it wherever possible. Their aversion to danger and discomfort leads them to play it safe. Extraverts, on the other hand, are highly sensitive to reward cues. They give more weight to the positives in a given course of action and downplay the negative possibilities. This can lead to impulsive or risk-taking behaviour. There seems to be good evidence that this dynamic was at play in the lead-up to the economic meltdown in 2008 when financial wheeler-dealers were throwing caution to the wind and making outrageous investment decisions and taking outsized risks.

Introverts see extraverts as impulsive. Extraverts see introverts as resistant to change, conservative, and willing to do anything to avoid pain. Extraverts are not particularly upset by conflict and may even seek it out, probably for its stimulating effect. I've been to dinner parties where someone will intentionally say something provocative to stir up a lively debate or even an argument. On one such occasion, it was the host who figuratively threw a firecracker into the conversation, then sat back and watched the fur fly. Meanwhile, his introverted wife was running around closing the windows, saying, "Benny, tone it down. The neighbours!"

Another Look at Motivation:
Biology Is Not the Only Factor

To what extent is temperament your destiny and to what extent do you have a choice?

Research indicates that introversion and extraversion are about 40 to 50 percent inherited. This means that biology isn't the whole story. This goes to the question of nature vs. nurture. Dr. Little suggests a distinction between "fixed traits" (our biological tendency toward intro- or extraversion) and "free traits" (a theory and term he developed to represent choices we make in certain situations to "act out of character"). "Free traits," he says, "are culturally scripted patterns of conduct that are strategically created to advance projects about which a person cares deeply." In other words, we're not just driven by our physiological dispositions; we're also motivated by our values, concerns, passions, projects, roles, and other acquired goals.

Dr. Little postulates that there are actually three determinants to our personality. He calls them our three "natures." Our first nature relates to our "biogenic traits," brain physiology and function that we're born with. Our second nature is our "sociogenic traits," different codes of behaviour according to the situation or context we find ourselves in: at school, at work, or socially. For example, there are times when even extraverts have to tone it down, such as at a birthday party—especially if it's in honour of someone other than them! Our third nature is what Dr. Little calls "free traits," which are based on choices we make to serve a greater cause or higher purpose. This is when we choose to "act out of character."

A Note of Caution

Dr. Little sounds an important note of caution about fixed traits. He warns against being too rigid in how we view our physiology. "You have to put fixed traits into perspective. Don't get caught in a dichotomous pigeonhole. Labelling can lead to self-fulfilling prophecies. The message is: Don't Trap Yourself."

So there is a yin and a yang here for you to be aware of. It's important to acknowledge your biogenic nature and to understand its implications. But it's equally important to recognize the element of flexibility and choice. You can, and often will, adopt "free traits" when it's meaningful for you to do so.

For example, as an introvert you might decide to join an environmental advocacy group to fight against pollution and climate change—possibly even becoming a spokesperson for the group. You could join Toastmasters to develop public speaking skills and increased comfort talking to large audiences in order to make presentations to business clients. You might accept a leadership role at work because you feel passionately about a new initiative they're rolling out. Like my friend Peter, you might choose to step outside your comfort zone to educate, inspire, and entertain students and audiences with the higher purpose of sharing the profound ideas that are so meaningful to you. Or you might choose to enter politics, an arena not for the faint of heart, because you feel passionately about civic or societal issues and want to make a significant contribution.

Here's a be-careful-what-you-wish-for story: An introverted friend of mine was a very successful behind-the-scenes person in a media company when she decided to write a book. The topic was very meaningful to her—the true story was amazing, the writing was beautiful, the messages and impact were profound, and the book became an international sensation. Then the real work started. The book was translated into forty languages and she was invited to speak all over the world. Being in the spotlight was uncomfortable enough for her, but public speaking was absolutely intimidating. However, it was important enough to her to share the lessons contained in the book's incredible story that she was willing to step way out of her comfort zone to achieve that goal. She summed up the experience this way: "It *cost* me a lot, but it *gave* me a lot."

Another example: Angela Kasner was a timid young girl who decided to study Russian. She did so well that her teacher encouraged her to enter competitions which involved role-playing various everyday situations. In this context, the more expressive students got higher marks from the judges. But being on stage and drawing attention to herself was both foreign to her and totally against her nature. In spite of her superior language skills, her performance was flat.

However, Angela also wanted to do well. So she forced herself to be more animated and expressive. As described in a March 2015 *Maclean's* article, "She somehow forced herself to be exuberant during competitions—speaking loudly, looking others in the eye and gesturing with her hands. None of it came naturally to her. She did it because she concluded it was necessary, because she wanted to win. And she did."

Later she decided to enter politics. "She recognizes what must be done and does it, whether it comes naturally to her or not," wrote journalist Mariam Lau in the newspaper *Die Zeit*. "It's absolutely not her style to lead. She doesn't like to lead. And still she has to do it. There's no one else." Today, that withdrawn young girl is the chancellor of Germany. We know her as Angela Merkel.

None of these examples are intended to imply that introverts have to overcome their shortcomings or "improve themselves" by becoming more like extraverts. They simply demonstrate that there are times when people are willing to leave their comfort zones to pursue a worthwhile goal.

There are also many situations in which extraverts choose to become more introverting to pursue a meaningful objective. They may be junior members of a committee who are asked to quietly sit in meetings and just observe or take notes. Or they might have just gotten married or had a baby and need to cut back on their active lifestyle and improve their abilities as good listeners to succeed in their spousal and parenting roles. One guy gave up his lively single life when he got married and had kids. Prior to settling down, his friends called him "Malibu Dave" because of the year-round suntan he acquired during his frequent travels. Later, Dave's wife would tease him when he was pushing a stroller or changing a diaper. "Gee, Malibu, if only your pals could see you now!" Dave had chosen to slow down in pursuit of a new and important goal.

CHAPTER 5

KNOW YOURSELF, ACHIEVE HARMONY

Rodgers and Hammerstein wrote a slew of legendary Broadway musicals, including *Oklahoma, South Pacific, Carousel*, and *The Sound of Music*. While Richard Rodgers wrote unforgettable melodies, Oscar Hammerstein crafted brilliant lyrics that conveyed both poetic beauty and keen insight. One of the most memorable songs from *The King and I* is "Getting to Know You." In terms of introversion and extraversion, this title is particularly apt. Self-awareness is the first step to learning to live in sync with yourself. I've encountered many people with introverting tendencies who never thought of themselves as introverts. They're shocked at the very notion or have simply never thought about it. They don't understand the biological basis of it, what the implications are, and how to manage themselves in light of their introverting preferences. Same with extraverts. They may realize they're outgoing but don't understand all the other ways their extraverting tendencies affect them.

To add to the confusion, sometimes introverts can fool themselves. They can behave in an outgoing fashion—for example, at a business convention or staff party—becoming "pseudo-extraverts." They may be indistinguishable from true extraverts to an outside observer. But they're paying a price internally. They may be oblivious to their internal states, failing to realize when they're overloading or feeling tension from conflict. Or they may ignore the signals, as so many people do with stress in general, accepting too much as being normal when it's actually excessive.

Or they may attribute the feelings to something else, such as a given situation or someone else's behaviour.

Other people can misread these situations as well. I attended a one-day seminar where the chairperson kept looking for the speaker at break time and couldn't find him. Attendees wanted to chat with the presenter and ask him questions. The host was perplexed that he'd disappeared. I immediately thought of Dr. Brian Little, a self-declared introvert who makes a point of disappearing during the breaks in his own high-energy program to lower his level of cortical arousal. He'll hide in the washroom or go for a walk at lunchtime. I shared this with the organizer, suggesting that the speaker may have been using the same strategy to quietly recharge his batteries during the intermission.

Here's another variation. It's also possible to be a "pseudo-introvert." These are natural extraverts who are constrained by role or situation to act in a circumspect, introverted manner. But they can only restrain themselves for so long. Then they need to escape and explode.

Understanding ourselves — how we feel and how we function — is a critical first step. But understanding others is also important. Whether they're family members, friends, neighbours, bosses, employees, coworkers, clients, or customers, being aware of their styles and preferences can lead to more respect, co-operation, productivity, and harmony. We could call this "Getting to Know *Me and You!*"

Incidentally, if I appear to be focusing more on understanding introverts, there are three reasons:

1. We live in a culture and society that seems to unfairly value extraverts more than introverts ("the extravert ideal").

2. I've seen so many patients make huge breakthroughs
    when they realized they were introverts and then made
    changes to adapt their lifestyles accordingly (more aware-
    ness leads to better choices).

3. There are a lot of misconceptions and judgements in our
    society about introverts that need to be corrected. These
    clarifications are validating and reassuring to introverts,
    and consciousness-raising for extraverts. And for both
    groups, it's about understanding and valuing the many
    strengths and benefits of introversion.

A Roundtable Discussion with Three Introverts

So with that in mind, let's eavesdrop on a conversation I organized around the breakfast table in our home with three unequiv-
ocal, self-aware introverts. I convened this meeting to learn more
about introverting characteristics and preferences. I put a tape
recorder in the middle of the table and asked one question: *What
would you like extraverts to know about introverts?* The insights
that came forth will be equally valuable to introverts who may
not be aware of their own tendencies.

The conversation began with a humorous and gentle rebuke
from one of the participants. Here's how it unfolded, followed
by excerpts from the discussion:

DAVID: As introverts, what would you want people to know
about you and about introversion? What have you learned about
yourself?

BOB: I think it's interesting that you chose to interview introverts in a group. [Laughter.] As an introvert, I thought you were going to interview each one of us individually, which would be the introvert's choice. Now this group is fine — we're all longtime friends — but put me in a different group of introverts and you might have long periods of silence.

SHERYL: I'd like people to know that we don't easily talk about ourselves, so you might want to ask us questions. Also, we tend toward deeper, more meaningful relationships as opposed to superficial relationships. We don't like a lot of small talk. We can do it, but we don't like it.

PAUL: I don't want to compete for time if I'm in a large group. If there's a person who is clearly very extraverting and comfortable holding the stage, I won't compete. I may think of funny things to say, or things that would be apt, but I won't compete. It's just not worth it.

It would be great if someone would turn to me and say, "So what do you think?" This is worse for me in situations where I don't know people. If I'm in a group of people whom I know very well, then I'm much more comfortable being spontaneous and initiating. With strangers, I am much more inclined to ask other people questions, so that oftentimes people will come away from a conversation saying, "I didn't hear anything about you." And I think, *Well, guess what? You didn't show that you were interested in what I thought.*

BOB: I had to learn some things about extraverting situations. It's like a list of skills when you go to a cocktail party or a social event. I hated them. I would want to disappear in a corner and not say anything. One of the first things I learned was to ask people about themselves. Most people want to talk about themselves. That's a way of opening the conversation. So, for me, as an introvert, being socialized was almost like social skills training, because I was such a strong introvert.

DAVID: If you say most people like to talk about themselves, is that a statement about people or mostly about extraverts, do you think?

BOB: I think introverts like to talk about themselves as well.

PAUL: If it's in a one-on-one situation. Introverting people often don't trust the first thing that comes into their mind. People who are extraverting talk to know what they think. I like to have time.

Let's say people are introducing themselves in a circle. I don't want to go first. I want time to think about what I am going to say and how I am going to present myself. It's about satisfying *myself.* It's not so much about impressing other people. It's about feeling that I represented myself the best I could to myself.

BOB: And I want to do it early on. If I'm in a group and we're asked a question, I want to say something and get it over with. Then I can just sit back and relax.

SHERYL: I would like the extraverts to know that the art of conversation means that both people speak. [Laughter.] And that often means, when you're speaking with an introvert, that it requires some effort on your part to listen.

BOB: And silence. I really appreciate when I have reached a level of comfort with a person where silence is acceptable.

PAUL: Also, in terms of physical space, I like privacy. If I'm at a party, what I want to find is a small, quiet, safe corner where I can talk to one person. I like quiet in order to hear someone, to listen to someone tell me things. I like to be able to close a door. That's why, I think, people of introverting preferences much prefer offices as opposed to open carrels. The idea of having a door to close, to have it to be quiet and private, is very important to me.

SHERYL: I would like extraverts to know that we tend to be reserved, we have a reserved façade, and they are not to misinterpret that as aloofness, being judgemental, or being stuck up. I've had that said about me.

BOB: What I experience is that people think I don't like them, I disapprove of them, that somehow I don't want to engage with them. And sometimes that's the truth, but other times it's not.

PAUL: It's people's discomfort with quiet again. If you're not seen to be moving out to engage, they think it means that you're standing back in judgement. I can't say that, as an introvert, when I see somebody doing that to me I don't have that same feeling as well. There are other times when I'm around another person who's introverting and I'm not getting very much from them and I'm thinking, *This person is highly introverting, but it's pretty opaque over there. I really don't know what they're thinking.* So I get that we can be kind of challenging.

I'm a fooler. Many people assume that I have an extraverting preference because I can be very outgoing. So I think they should pay attention to what people say about their desire to spend long periods of time with others. That is, I'm constantly looking for ways to get out of social situations. *OK, I'm here. I'm going to stay for half an hour.* How can I find a socially acceptable way to look at my watch and say, "Ooh, I've been here for half an hour. Gotta move on!" And oftentimes, people with an extraverting preference take that personally: "He doesn't like us. He wants to get away. Blah blah blah." So if people with extraverting preferences could be curious, rather than judgemental, about something that looks as though it's being antisocial or judgemental, and say, "Gee, I wonder if, actually, he's exhausted. I wonder if he's just overwhelmed. I wonder if he's just had enough. This isn't about us."

And oftentimes, people who have extraverting preferences don't want to let you go. "No, stay and have another drink." I don't want to do that. I have spent hours trying to find socially acceptable ways to say, "I can't take this anymore. I'm just done. I gotta get out of here. And don't take this personally. It isn't about you."

The best way to learn about other people is to talk to them. Ask them questions, and then really listen to their answers. Introversion isn't well understood because it's not talked about much—and introverts don't talk about *themselves* much either. That's why I convened this panel and taped the discussion. It's one thing to learn about people from reading, but it's far more instructive to hear about their lived experience in their own words.

CHAPTER 6

CLARIFYING SOME MISCONCEPTIONS

Distinctions and Connections: A Q&A with Dr. Brian Little

DAVID: Is there a difference between introversion and shyness?

DR. LITTLE: Yes, and the distinction is important. Whereas shy people *want* to interact with others, they feel unable to do so. Socializing is uncomfortable and stressful for them, so they avoid it. It has to do with social anxiety. Introverts, on the other hand, *enjoy* socializing with others but find too much of it to be overwhelming and draining. They don't want too much interaction. Professor Bernardo Carducci, a shyness expert at Indiana University Southeast, puts it this way: "The shy want desperately to connect but find socializing difficult. Introverts seek alone time because they want time alone." In an article in *Psychology Today*, Dr. Laurie Helgoe says that both types might be standing on the sidelines at a party, but the introvert prefers to be there while the shy person feels she has no choice.

DAVID: Is there a relationship between attention deficit hyperactivity disorder (ADHD) and extraversion?

DR. LITTLE: Yes, there is. If one agreed with Dr. Hans Eysenck's view of extraversion, those with ADHD would be regarded as extremely extraverted individuals who need stimulation to get up to an optimal level of arousal (OLA). Parents are often confused about why physicians prescribe Ritalin, a stimulant, when their kids are already going up the wall—seemingly overstimulated. The answer is that the stimulant creates an artificial increase in arousal to an optimal level so that the kid doesn't *need* to climb the walls to get to that optimal level.

DAVID: Is there a relationship between extraversion and type A behaviour?

DR. LITTLE: No. Despite the fact that a lot of type A people are driven and always on the go, and seem very outgoing, there is apparently no correlation between that behaviour and extraversion. They are similar but not the same.

DAVID: Do introverts have more trouble with insomnia than extraverts?

DR. LITTLE: Yes, they do. Again, there is over-arousal in the ascending reticular formation and projections into the prefrontal areas. As a certified introvert, I cannot have coffee after 6 p.m. and expect to get a good sleep. Alcohol helps, but, as you know, rebounds at 3 a.m. make that less helpful than great sex and/ or meditation. However, introverts may have a compensatory advantage according to a recent study of military personnel. It showed that introverts function better than extraverts when they're sleep deprived.

DAVID: (My wife amazes me at how well she functions when she doesn't sleep well. When that happens to me, I feel like a zombie wandering around in a haze.)

Are there changes in introversion and extraversion across the lifespan?

DR. LITTLE: Over time, and linked to testosterone levels, extraversion decreases in males. Although the data on this are more complex, women tend to show no such drop. I think it is because in later life, women are able to adopt pseudo-extraverted characteristics so that outgoing behaviour becomes more normative. It does mean that at midlife, men decrease their extraversion and women increase theirs. This can lead to some potentially perplexing marital implications.

CHAPTER 7

WHAT NOW?

The question for you, the reader, is: What do I do with all this information? What are the implications for me as an individual and for my relationships with other people?

The first step is to locate yourself somewhere along the introversion-extraversion continuum. We all have characteristics of both tendencies but usually one predominates. Are you a strong introvert or do you have mild introverting preferences? Are you an intense extravert, or do you have milder extraverting tendencies? Put your X somewhere on this spectrum.

$$\longleftarrow \hspace{5cm} \longrightarrow$$

INTROVERT   **AMBIVERT**   **EXTRAVERT**

Again, please note that these preferences are not hard-and-fast labels. They are offered as useful guides to help you better understand yourself and others.

Once you've identified your preference, here are some tips to guide the way you behave and manage your energy:

For Introverts:

1. **Tune into your body and watch for signs of overload.**
   There will be times when you enjoy lively interaction or being at a party. But the time will come when you've had enough.

What are the symptoms or signals that tell you "I'm done?"
Let's listen in again on my breakfast table panel discussing
this question:

BOB: I sometimes get bored—or I begin to get sleepy or
distracted. I start looking at something in the room and
away from the person who's talking to me.

SHERYL: I start to feel inside—I can't even describe it.
It's kind of like a top—and I wouldn't show it physically.
[Quick inhalation-type gasps.] It's kind of like *that*. I'm
overstimulated.

PAUL: I can feel myself getting very irritable, even angry.
Tense, like I'm going to jump out of my skin. It really is
a sense of having reached the threshold.

SHERYL: Tuning out.

PAUL: Exhaustion. Just simple exhaustion.

BOB: For me, being able to listen is really important.
And when I feel like I can no longer listen, I know I have
to leave.

PAUL: One of the cues for me is that even the people that
I *care* about I don't care about anymore. All I want to do
is get out of there.

Identify what signals you get from *your* body and mind when
you've reached your limit of stimulation and feel overloaded.

2. **Be proactive. Pace yourself. Plan ahead.**

Plan time-outs at certain intervals throughout the day, and especially after meetings or intense interactive activities. Plan your social calendar so you go out once or twice a week — depending on your tolerance — and space these events out (not back-to-back evenings.) Go out for dinner or a movie, but not both. Decide how long to stay at family gatherings and then give yourself permission to leave — or arrive a bit late to shorten your stay.

3. **Develop restorative strategies and resources.**

Find ways to lower your state of arousal. In their excellent book, *The Power of Full Engagement,* Jim Loehr and Tony Schwartz discuss "recovery rituals and routines." It might be a nap or a hot bubble bath. It might be completing a crossword puzzle, playing the guitar, listening to music, reading a magazine, doing needlepoint. It could be meditating, taking a walk, looking out the window, or just daydreaming for a few minutes. At a party, you might go outside or wander down the hall for a short break. Develop a range of strategies that you can employ in different situations.

> The price for not taking time out to indulge your natural inclinations is stress and eventual burnout.

4. **Let people know when you're not receptive to interaction.**

You may be busy working on a report, reading, thinking, or just in recovery mode to bring down your cortical arousal level. Other people may not appreciate that you're in the middle of something and try to interrupt you or start up a conversation. (These are probably extraverts who are trying to get their own arousal levels *up*!) Find ways to indicate that you're not "open for business" at the moment. Subtle gestures like closing your door or not looking up may be enough. Someone I know puts earphones on when travelling on the commuter train—even though the sound on her iPod is turned off. If other people are less sensitive (or frankly *unconscious*—and there are many of those around), you may have to be more direct. For example, say, "Forgive me, but I'm in the middle of something right now. Can we talk later?"

5. **Let people know when you're thinking.**
Introverts think before they speak. This can confuse extraverts who might assume you're ignoring them. If you haven't fully formulated your thoughts yet, explain your silence to them. Tell them you're considering the issue or just need a moment to digest what they've said. In addition, be willing to verbalize your thoughts more—to show that you're reflecting on the matter—and share some of those thoughts.

6. **Tell extraverts when you're overloaded.**
Conversations between extraverts and introverts are like an energy exchange. Extraverts talk to boost their energy, but often this is at the expense of an introverted listener who is drained by the experience. After a while the introvert feels not only saturated but *used* by the "energy vampire" monologuing at them. The extravert is loving the (too-often one-way) exchange and is probably oblivious to the effect it's having on you. Tell them when you've had enough—and why. Raise their consciousness. Increase their awareness about introversion

and extraversion. This is especially important if you're in a close or long-term relationship with an extravert, be it at work, at home, or in your social circle. If you do it kindly and

> A conversation between an extravert and an introvert is like an energy exchange. The extravert gets energized— but at the expense of the introvert, who is drained by the experience.

diplomatically, both of you will benefit from your candour.

7. **Be open to social opportunities.**
   Don't become a recluse. Find compatible people to spend time with. Go to parties, especially smaller gatherings, and expose yourself to enjoyable activities. Most introverts can be outgoing in moderation—and miss out on their full potential (not to mention a lot of fun) if they hide or overprotect themselves too much.

8. **Be willing to step out of your comfort zone in the pursuit of goals that are important to you.**
   Exercise your "free traits" to work toward meaningful personal projects that you feel passionate about. But remember to pace yourself. Stepping out of character for too long can lead to excessive stress or even burnout.

9. **Don't judge yourself.**
   Understand the basis of introversion and acknowledge that you can't change the way

> Don't let extraverts define or judge your reality.

your brain is wired. If excess stimulation exhausts you, that's just the way it is. Don't feel guilty or "less than" if social situations wear you out.

10. **Use alcohol and caffeine mindfully.**
Remember that alcohol has a sedating effect and may actually help to calm the brain activity of introverts. Conversely, caffeine is a stimulant and will jack up the cortical arousal of introverts who may already be above their optimal level of arousal. If you like feeling wired, forget drugs like ecstasy and just grab a cup of java from your neighbourhood coffee shop.

For Extraverts:

Let me be clear. Extraverts are not "the bad guys." They have issues too — with managing their energy or feeling rebuffed when introverts don't want to engage with them. It's important for extraverts to be understood by others and by themselves. More awareness leads to better choices — for everyone.

1. **Monitor your energy level and know when and how to increase it.**
If you're starting to fade, take a break to "wake yourself up." Get up and move around. Call a friend or chat with a colleague. Go for a walk or run. Watch a funny video on YouTube. Turn on some music. Go to a store or cafeteria where there are people and activity. Go to where the action is.

2. **Check out whether people are "open for business."**

   Don't impose yourself on others if they're not receptive. Ask if they've got a few minutes to chat. Watch for clues that they may not be amenable to company: they're reading or preoccupied, not making eye contact, or not engaging when you start to talk to them. Be more aware of when you may be interrupting or intruding. And don't be offended if they seem uninterested. They may be in the middle of serious thought or just trying to recharge their energy by being quiet. It might have nothing to do with you.

3. **Ask for permission before using someone as a sounding board.**

   Extraverts like to talk through problems and bounce ideas off others. But don't assume that they're willing to be your audience. Say something like "I'm working on a proposal and I'm feeling a bit stuck. Do you mind if I run this by you?" Or "I'm having some trouble with Murray and was wondering if you'd give me some feedback about how to approach him."

4. **Know when you're overstaying your welcome.**

   Introverts are good listeners, but there's a limit. Monitor yourself and come up for air. Don't drone on and on. Be sensitive to when you're overloading them. They may be reluctant to tell you outright, so watch for clues. When their eyes glaze over, you've probably lost them. When they take a sudden interest in the carpet, you might want to desist. If they seem a bit irritated or exasperated, shut it down. Again, don't take it personally, but acknowledge that you've drained them. Conversation should be a dialogue, not a monologue. Be proactive. Don't wait for the other person to show a lack of interest or displeasure before you pause and give them a chance to speak.

5. **Ask questions and listen more.**
   Ask introverts questions and then listen attentively and actively with occasional words such as "aha" or "I see." This is especially relevant in talking to introverts who don't easily initiate conversation or talk about themselves. Be genuinely interested in learning about others and hearing their opinions.

6. **Give introverts time to think and space to recover their energy.**
   Don't jump in when introverts are quietly contemplating what you've said or the question you've asked. Extraverts often fill silences by starting to talk again. Resist the temptation. Similarly, give them space to be alone and quiet when they need solitude and silence.

7. **Don't talk too much or interrupt when others are talking.**
   This is especially important with introverts who may have been reticent about speaking. If you interrupt, they might just shut down again. This is especially important in meetings and group discussions. (It's relevant with extraverts too, but they won't *let* you interrupt — or they may just interrupt *your* interruption!) Also, don't jump in to take back the floor. Avoid interjections such as "Yeah, I had that experience too" or "That reminds of the time when…" followed by you telling another story.

8. **Beware of making impulsive decisions.**
   Don't jump too quickly when making important decisions that involve elements of risk. Be willing to listen to considered words of caution from introverts when contemplating such matters.

9. **Don't pressure or guilt-trip introverts to be more sociable.**
   If someone says they don't like crowded, noisy restaurants or large dinner parties, take them at their word. If they don't want to attend their high school reunion, don't try to shame them into it. If they choose to leave a cocktail party early because they're drained and have had enough, don't lean on them to stay longer. And don't embarrass them by calling attention to their early departure. This is especially important advice for parents and teachers when dealing with introverting children. Pushing them to be extraverts will only increase their discomfort and stress level and send a signal that they're not OK just the way they are.

10. **Use alcohol and caffeine mindfully.**
    Remember that alcohol has a sedating effect and may push the slow-revving extravert to an even lower level of arousal— if not outright stupor! Alcohol on a working day or when you want to make a good impression on a client would not be wise—unless you think heavy eyelids will seal the deal you're working on. On the other hand, caffeine is a stimulant and, if used strategically and judiciously, may improve your level of cortical arousal and performance.

For Both Groups:

Above all, be true to yourself. Determine your predisposition, design your life to suit your introverting or extraverting preference, and have the courage of your convictions. Stop fighting your biology and trying to be what you're not. And if you choose to step out of character to pursue a higher goal or value, do so mindfully. Proceed with full awareness

> Seek to be congruent, and "to thine own self be true."

of what you're doing and why you're doing it, and monitor yourself for signs that you need to restore your energy in ways that are appropriate for your innate trait.

Three final thoughts to keep in mind:

- Understand and recognize the differences in personality traits and preferences.

- Honour and respect the differences—in yourself and in others.

- Celebrate the differences. We all need each other.

SECTION 2

NATURAL TIME
VS.
ARTIFICIAL TIME

CHAPTER 8

OUR RACE AGAINST TIME

It's a cloudy day in May. I'm a junior in high school and have made it to the suburban Toronto track finals in the half mile. I'm one of ten runners from forty-four schools and I'm nervous beyond words. We get to the starting line and — BANG — the gun goes off. We sprint the first fifty yards to get a position on the inside lane. I settle in and think to myself, *Hey, this may turn out OK!*

Coming into the last two hundred yards, I go into my final kick. On the last curve, I'm in third place. Just then, a teammate on the infield yells out to me, "Ya better hurry — they're running up your tail." In trying to quicken my pace for one last push, I lose my rhythm, miss a step, and stumble. In that moment, four runners roar past me. I finish seventh. Even though my time is a personal best, I feel crushed.

I learned an important lesson that day: when you're going as fast as you can, you simply can't go any faster.

Fast-forward a dozen years. I am now a young doctor working in a medical clinic. One of the senior physicians wants me to see more patients. He wants me to work faster. He volunteers to share his wisdom on how to best achieve this. The conversation goes something like this:

"What do you say when you walk into the examining room?"

"I say, 'Good morning. I'm Dr. Posen. How can I help you?'"

"Alright, let's stop right there. First of all, you don't have to say 'good morning.' Second, you don't have to tell them who you are. They know who's going to see them. Third, just get right to the point."

"Well, what do *you* do?" I ask him.

"I walk in and ask, 'What's the problem?'"

"How elegant," I muse, ironically. "Why didn't *I* think of that? Gee, by being abrupt, I could probably save four or five minutes every day!" I politely thank him for his mentoring and get back to my work.

There were several reasons why I didn't follow his advice and chose instead to work at a more comfortable pace:

1. Patients don't like to be rushed in and out of the office.

2. Patients need time to tell their story.

3. If I hurry, I run the risk of missing important details and making mistakes.

4. It's tiring and stressful to go fast all day long; it's easier when you pace yourself.

5. Medicine is an art as well as a science — it involves listening, sensitivity, and connecting with patients.

6. It's much more satisfying. I was a family physician for seventeen years. What I enjoyed most about my work was the people. If I'd rushed through my days — and years — I would have missed so much of the quality of the relationships I developed with my patients.

We all have to make choices about how fast we want to live our lives. We all have to choose how much speeding up we're willing to buy into. Wherever possible in our work lives, we should find a tempo that feels right for us — in terms of both efficiency and comfort. While, in some jobs, the speed is dictated by machinery or group norms, in most jobs there's room for variability.

In our nonwork lives, we have more freedom to choose — and to speak up when the pace becomes unacceptable. I know a woman who finally stood up to her frenetic type A husband, who was always overloading his schedule, trying to squeeze in one more thing and dashing from one activity to another. One night, after a hurried restaurant meal before rushing off to a movie, she put her foot down. "I'm not inhaling my food and getting indigestion anymore. We go out either for dinner or to a movie, but not both unless we have at least two hours to enjoy a relaxing meal."

We're living in an age of high speed. Everything's going faster — except rush hour traffic, service in retail stores, lineups at airports, and a few other modern delights. Titles of books reflect this: *Overwhelmed: Work, Love, and Play When No One Has the Time*; *Thank You for Being Late: An Optimist's Guide to Thriving in the Age of Accelerations*; and *CrazyBusy* among them. While some people embrace this trend, many others struggle with it. It's a huge source of stress. Overload has become an epidemic. Folks complain they have too much to do and not enough time. But most of us feel we have no choice — so we just pedal harder and faster to keep up. It's time for a little pushback. A hit Broadway show in 1966 was titled *Stop the World — I Want to Get Off*. It's a sentiment many people share.

Examples of Our Hurry-Up Culture

- Twitter's 140 characters

- instant messaging

- sound bites on radio and TV

- media multitasking, such as CNN's News Crawler

- fast food (now you can scarf down your meal, prepare it in a blender, or nuke it in a microwave)

- speed-reading (Woody Allen on taking a speed-reading course: "I read *War and Peace* in twenty minutes. It's about Russia.")

- speed dating (a more efficient way to pick your life's partner?)

- convenience stores at gas stations called "On the Run"

- running yellow lights (no longer do amber lights mean "prepare to stop" — they mean "better hurry up")

- oxymoronic phrases such as "rush hour" (it should be called "snail hour" or "gridlock hour," though it's more like three to four hours — *twice a day!*)

- acronyms (who would waste time saying "Hall of Fame" when you can say "HoF" instead?)

MY FAVOURITE ACRONYM STORY involves a twenty-eight-year-old guy admitted to hospital for a surgical procedure. The diagnosis on his chart says CHF. In medical circles, this means "congestive heart failure."

The nurse on the floor takes one look at this healthy, strapping young man and says: "There seems to be a mistake here. This guy looks perfectly well."

The admitting clerk replies: "No, there's no mistake. He's here to have a circumcision!"

CHF means "changing his faith."

There are three things to note here:

- Speed is accelerating all around us.

- We're allowing ourselves to be caught up in it.

- It's very stressful for a lot of people.

CHAPTER 9

HOW DID THIS HAPPEN?
A HISTORY LESSON

Natural Time vs. Artificial Time

How did all this happen? How did we get here? Jeremy Rifkin offered some compelling answers in his provocative book *Time Wars*. When I first encountered this book, I was surprised by the subtitle, "The Primary Conflict in Human History." That seemed like a rather over-the-top bit of marketing hype—until I started reading. Rifkin argues persuasively that our struggles with time began with our disconnection from natural, biological time. Human beings created a completely artificial way of reckoning and measuring time, which later led to perversions of its use. Now this artificial system runs our lives, with chilling consequences.

People spent most of human history living by the organic rhythms of nature: the seasons, the lunar month, the solar day. Life was guided by the regularly changing seasons, the tides, sunrise and sunset, phases of the moon, animal and bird migrations. Examples of biological time in nature abound: roosters crow at dawn, plants extend their leaves during daylight hours and fold them at night, orca whales swim up and down the Pacific coast at specific times of year between North and South America. An example cited in *Time Wars* is the fascinating annual migration of the swallows of a small Catholic mission near Los Angeles. The birds leave the mission every year on the same day, October 23rd, and fly to Argentina for the winter. They return every spring precisely on March 19th. In a span of two hundred years, they have been late only twice! This remarkable example of biological time was immortalized in the popular love song "When the Swallows Come Back to Capistrano."

Our human bodies function on a similar biological basis. We have all kinds of internal body clocks, including day-night wake-sleep cycles, appetite cycles, monthly menstrual cycles, seasonal mood fluctuations, etc. We carried on as a species for thousands of years, following the ebbs and flows of nature and living in accordance with its multiple rhythms.

THE FIRST INDICATION of the existence of endogenous circadian rhythms was reported in 1729 by French astronomer Jean de Marain. He knew that plants extended their leaves during the daylight hours and folded them at night. Marain was quite surprised, however, to find that certain plants would continue to open and shut their leaves at the appropriate time, even when kept in total darkness.

The History of Time Measurement

And then along came the concept of reckoning "time." And that's when the trouble started, although not initially. It began innocently enough with simple organizing principles such as when to sleep, when to hunt and fish, and — with the advent of agriculture — when to plant and reap crops. Over time, and as people began living in tribes and larger groups, the concept of cultural or societal time evolved. Market days, feast days, and

"No sooner had I learned to tell time than I began arriving late everywhere."
— Jane Wagner

holy days emerged, often tied to primitive religions that were based largely on nature. The "year" was based on the earth's orbit around the sun, the "month" was based on the phases of the moon, and the "day" reflected one full rotation of the Earth on its axis. All the other measurements were arbitrary, human constructs. The "week" originated as the interval of time between market days—and varied in length between three and ten days. The "hour" was later invented as a unit to divide up the solar day, and somewhere along the line, it was decided that there would be twenty-four of them in a day. Why twenty-four and not twenty or ten remains a mystery.

In the mid-seventeenth century, the "minute" was devised as a way of further dividing time into more precise units. Again, the choice of breaking up an hour into sixty minutes seems strictly discretionary. Why not twenty-four again, or one hundred? Maybe they just anticipated that in three hundred years Don Hewitt and Mike Wallace would choose to name their Sunday-night television program 60 Minutes.

By the early 1700s, someone sliced and diced time measurement even further. The second hand was added to the clock, dividing each minute into sixty parts (the number sixty was really catching on). In the twentieth century, seconds were further subdivided (this time by ten). Very handy for track meets and ski races. Then quartz timekeeping allowed further subdivisions to hundredths of a second. Not to be outdone, computers refined the process to thousandths of a second. Now we have the ultimate measurement: the nanosecond. That's one billionth of a second. We can now measure time in units so tiny that we can't even experience them. The snap of a finger takes 500 million nanoseconds. We have laser accuracy, but what's the point of it all? And, more important, what is the cost?

We have gone from natural, biological time to artificial time. That arbitrary human construct have taken us from cultural time to clock time to computer time. With this increasingly sophisticated ability to measure time has come changes in the rhythms of society, including the accelerated tempo of our high-speed, fast-paced, 24/7 culture. It is totally at odds with the way our bodies are designed, and with the way people lived for most of human history.

CHAPTER 10

THE TWO FUNCTIONS OF TIME

Before we explore the costs and consequences of our time-driven, ever-faster world, let's look at a fundamental question: What is the purpose of time and being able to measure it so precisely? The first function is *efficiency*. Planning is indispensable for social organization and order. It provides a way to ensure predictability. The second is *control*—which can often lead to *power*. This is where the problems come from.

> "Time is nature's way of keeping everything from happening at once."
> —Woody Allen

Efficiency

Consider the story of Scottish engineer Sir Sandford Fleming. In Ireland in July 1876, he missed a train bound for Londonderry because every local jurisdiction had its own system of time measurement, often uncoordinated with other local municipalities. Kind of hard to run a railroad that way! Most travellers would probably just wait for the next train, but this inconvenience got Fleming thinking. There had to be a better way to organize rail travel. Thus began a brilliant process of innovative thinking that led to a much bigger solution—one with implications that affect us to this day.

Fleming proposed the standardization of time. The shift from local mean time (LMT) to the standard time system removed confusion and frustration for travellers. It was adopted by the railroads in 1883 and by most states almost immediately after. Eventually it was used worldwide. It led to the division of the globe into twenty-four hourly units (or "time zones") with the prime meridian placed in Greenwich, England (Greenwich Mean Time). For his genius and far-ranging thinking, Fleming was knighted by Queen Victoria.

Regulated time started to be used to organize societal activities such as market days when buyers and sellers knew they could come together for mutual benefit. Time schedules help us to organize events, activities, and our lives in general.

Artificial time is based on purely social conventions. Think of the week. During the Industrial Revolution, people worked six days a week, with only Sunday off as a day of rest. The workday was once fourteen hours out of every twenty-four. Then it was reduced to twelve, then ten, and finally, in the twentieth century, the eight-hour day became standard. The public school year begins in September and ends in June. But that's starting to morph into an August start time in many jurisdictions. Most universities finish classes in April and hold exams in May. The academic year is divided up into semesters. It's all arbitrarily constructed. We have "lunch hour," "dinnertime," and — everyone's favourite — "happy hour"!

Other examples of artificial time serving the cause of efficiency include timetables, work schedules, and starting times for games, concerts, and social functions. We book appointments for the hairdresser, tee-off times for golf, a time to meet friends for lunch. This human construct serves us well when it helps us to organize our daily activities — without conflicting with our normal biological rhythms and internal body clocks. So far, so good.

Control and Power

But it didn't take long for mankind (and it was men who did this) to figure out that they could use time to control the behaviour of others. And that's when the mischief and misery really began.

I saw this indirectly through one of my patients. Brenda always booked my first appointment slot of the day for her counselling sessions. Our 8 a.m. start time allowed her to get to work just after 9 and avoid incurring the wrath of her dictatorial boss. One morning we were heavily into an important issue so I extended the visit. But Brenda was getting increasingly agitated and started to check her watch frequently. She finally explained her dilemma: while Brenda appreciated the extra time, she had become preoccupied with the fear of being late for work and having to deal with an angry boss. Here we were trying to reduce her stress, but the arbitrary start time at her office was *generating* stress. We had to stop so she could get on her way.

The kicker was that this woman was in sales. When "checking in," all she had to do was pick up her schedule and a few samples. But her boss insisted that she show up "on time" before she went out on the road to see customers. Upon leaving the head office, her time was her own and nobody monitored her hour-by-hour activities. She wasn't relieving a shift worker or working on an assembly line where everyone had to work together. But she was put under enormous pressure to appear at this artificially set time. It's as if her boss just wanted to remind her who was in control.

It's not hard to guess how the phrase "punching the clock" came about. I suspect that a lot of these new devices were attacked by human fists, so pervasive was their diabolical power.

Other Examples of Control

1. **School bells**
   Do you remember racing the last few blocks to school when you thought you'd be late? Or scrambling to get from one class to another before the bell rang? Do you think the school was wielding a bit of power there? The penalty for lateness was usually a detention, which, at my high school, was served at 8 a.m. This always amused me because if someone was having trouble getting to school by 9, what chance would they have of showing up on time for their detention an hour earlier?

2. **Work schedules**
   This ups the ante on the school-bell issue because the punishments are more significant. Reprimands, docking of pay, demotions, or even being fired are all possible consequences of tardiness, especially if it's chronic.

3. **Deadlines**
   Deadlines for assignments, reports, projects, and other deliverables are another form of control—at school but especially in the workplace. And the pace has been ramping up for years. Just in the last decade, people went from complaining about "tight" deadlines to beefing about "unrealistic" deadlines. Now they often lament about "impossible" deadlines. Who's setting these ridiculous time frames that are frazzling so many employees? The people with the power, that's who!

4. **Timed exams**
   We've all written tests and exams that had a specified length—one hour, two hours, three hours. But when I was

in medical school, there was a fiendish variation of limited testing time: it was called the "bell ringer" exam. This is where you walked into a room filled with exhibits on counters. Each specimen had a stool in front of it. Everyone started at a different "station" where they had one minute to examine a bone or a specimen under a microscope and answer questions about it. Then a bell would ring and you'd move on to the next position where there was another artifact to examine and answer questions about. This continued until we'd all visited each exhibit.

It was like musical chairs—although there were enough seats for everyone. Every sixty seconds there was a mad scramble to finish the questions and move on to the next seat. It got really interesting if the person ahead of you hadn't vacated their seat on time and you wasted precious seconds waiting to get started. I never saw any fistfights or forcible removals, but there were many testy moments of impatience and frustration. Above all, it was *very* stressful! People moved, thought, and wrote at different speeds (even if they knew all the answers). The relentless minideadlines and infernal racket of ringing bells only added to the dynamic. Whether it was a good way to test students' knowledge I don't know, but as a formula for manufacturing adrenalin, it was hard to beat. This is the atmosphere of many hurried workplaces, whether on assembly lines or at grocery checkout counters. Employers now have the technology to count key strokes for people working on computers and to measure how fast items are scanned at supermarkets. How's that for relentless pressure and the exercise of power?

The factory was the first place where people were exposed to the modern schedule. In the new factory system, machinery dictated the tempo. Assembly lines were timed to move at a certain pace and everyone had to keep up. A worker might only have a few seconds to turn a screw or use a wrench. If he coughed or sneezed, that might be enough to keep him scrambling to catch up. The pursuit for ultimate efficiency in such workplaces created a true tyranny of time.

Once the concept of working faster became ingrained, the language started to reflect the culture: from Benjamin Franklin's "time is money" to *"tempus fugit"* ("time is fleeting"). Today, every sector is driven by its own mantra:

- Factory production lines: "keep it moving"

- Corporate: "gotta increase market share"; "gotta grow the company"

- Lawyers and accountants: "billable hours"

- Doctors: "get 'em in, get 'em out"

It's all about speed and having more. Phrases such as "growth is good" and "more is better" seem to capture this sentiment. In *The Age of Speed*, Vince Poscente says we're living in an age of "more/faster/now."

To summarize, once the concept of time was firmly in place, people found that it had a useful purpose in helping to organize society — the *efficiency* function. Then came the unintended consequences. Some folks noticed they could use time to *control* the behaviour of other people. After that, it was only a short leap to the realization that there was real *power* in being able to do so. That's when the race to exploit others really began, starting in the Industrial Revolution. The drive for money and power was on in earnest and it has never let up. Whenever there's a buck to be made, human beings will find a way to pursue and exploit it. As technology improved, the race got faster. Finally, computer technology ramped us up to warp speed, which is where we are now.

We've become a speeded-up, time-hurried, type A, driven, impatient society, rushing around in a race against the clock. A *Herman* cartoon captures this beautifully. It shows a man getting into a taxi. But he's opening the *driver's* door. As the bewildered cabbie looks up, the man says, "I gotta be at the airport in three minutes. I'm driving!"

CHAPTER 11

COSTS AND CONSEQUENCES: WHY SHOULD YOU CARE?

The conflict between biological and clock time takes many forms. Take a look at high school students waiting for the bus in the morning. Do they look lively and animated? Do they look happy and cheerful? Hardly! They look like disconnected zombies, sullen and exhausted, eyelids at half-mast. This is what teachers look at during first period every day.

Why are these teenagers half-asleep at 7:30 in the morning? Because their brains *are* asleep. It has to do with something called "phase shift delay" in the wake-sleep cycle, a phenomenon that begins in adolescence and lasts into the early twenties. Simply put, these teens wind down later in the evening than adults do, and they don't wake up until later in the morning. This is a function of physiology; it's biological. This subject will be explored further in the section on sleep.

These young people are not lazy slugs. It's just that they're being asked to wake up in the middle of the night (so to speak) because of a societal, artificial construct called "the school schedule," which is totally at odds with their normal body rhythms.

It also relates to another clock-time arrangement called "the school busing schedule." Many elementary and high school students are ferried to school by bus. They can't all be transported at once. So it was decided to move the teens out in the first run and then go back to carry the younger children. Ironically, this is exactly the opposite of what should be done. Little kids naturally wake up earlier than teens. But societal decisions were made for administrative reasons that are not only unrelated to biology but in direct conflict with it.

Only humans impose a social sense of time on top of the biological clocks that exist within us. Cultural and social time clash head-on with our biological and natural time.

Shift work is another example of the body's internal rhythms being jolted out of sync by the radical time changes our bodies are forced to adjust to. The disruption of natural rhythms leads to all kinds of health, relationship, and safety problems.

And then there's jet lag. Travelling from Europe to America in less than a day would have astonished Christopher Columbus. (Talk about being born too soon!) But the other side of the miracle of flight is the biological discombobulation that throws off your sleep cycle, interferes with digestion, and disrupts the rhythm of many other bodily functions. It can take days to adjust to the new time zone, depending on the distance travelled. The formula is roughly one day of adjustment for every hour of time-zone change.

What Is Our Speeded-Up Society Costing Us?

1. **We're losing time to reflect.**
   Technology has accelerated time dramatically. One critical thing that's been lost is the time to think about things. We have less time for contemplation, for stepping back to gain perspective. A veteran lawyer described the evolution of newer and faster communication. He remembers the old days, when he'd receive letters from clients or other lawyers would ask his opinion about a legal matter. He would think about it and dictate a letter back to them. Then came the fax

machine. He'd get the same letter by fax, but now it would say, "Can you get back to me by two o'clock today?" Then it was email, asking for a reply within an hour. Finally, it was the smartphone and text message, with the expectation of an answer almost immediately. There was a sense of urgency. What's lost is the time to contemplate, to consider all aspects of an issue, and to then formulate a cogent, thoughtful response.

2. **We're losing our patience.**
Stories abound about people receiving a text message on their smartphone — then another one, minutes later, asking, "Did you get my message? I haven't heard from you yet." Long lineups and slow service send people into orbit. Folks are often in such a hurry these days that they feel they can't stop to chat for a few minutes if they run into an old friend on the street.

HERE'S A CAUTIONARY TALE: A conscientious lawyer made a point of returning phone calls on the same day they were received. Even on vacation, his voice message said he would return calls before the end of each business day. On one such occasion, he called a client back as promised — only to be told that they couldn't wait that long to speak to him, so they'd found and hired another lawyer.

3. **We're becoming less efficient.**
There's an old saying that "haste makes waste." When we hurry, we're more likely to overlook things and make mistakes. We tend to make rushed, impulsive decisions. We

don't have time to check emails or reports that might contain errors (the autocorrect function on computers might mean well, but it sure leads to a lot of misspelled and misinterpreted words). In factories and manual work, hurrying also increases the risk of accidents and injuries.

4. **We're unable to do our jobs properly.**
Hospital nurses have always prided themselves on being caring professionals who not only monitor patients, administer medications, and change dressings, but also spend time with patients and genuinely care for—and about—these sick people. Due to cutbacks and increased bureaucratic expectations, nurses have been under enormous pressure to work faster and tend to more—and more acutely ill—patients while doing more charting and paperwork. The frustration at not being able to do their job the way they know it could and should be done has led to more stress and lower feelings of engagement and satisfaction.

5. **We have less time for leisure, for sleep, for exercise, for each other!**
Ironically, back in the 1950s, magazine articles talked about the anticipated challenges people would face when technology allowed them to work part-time and what they would do with so much leisure time. That's one pipe dream that got shattered! Ironically, we have *less* free time today. There's a very instructive cartoon in the series *Between Friends* that shows a woman zooming through a park at full speed, clutching her briefcase. She then slows down, stops, looks around at the flowers and beauty surrounding her, and says with a wide-eyed and slightly sad face, "Wow! Will you look at that?

And I always thought it was *life* that was rushing past *me*."

One of the biggest complaints on employee surveys in the past twenty years has been a lack of work-life balance. During the downsizing frenzy in the mid-1990s, people started working harder and faster to keep up with the expanded workload left to the remaining staff. When that didn't work, they began working longer hours to get everything done. This trend has now become ingrained. People work longer hours than they did twenty years ago—and they are still running faster just to keep up. So much for the rosy predictions from the 1950s!

6. **We're becoming chronically stressed out.**
   A major result of this ramped-up pace is more stress, frayed nerves, and more sickness. People are cranky; muscles are tense. Simply put: working longer, harder, and faster isn't working anymore. Collectively, we've hit a wall. The fastest growing sector of disability insurance claims is for stress-related illnesses, including anxiety, depression, and burnout. If that's the price of prosperity, it's a lousy trade-off.

Connecting the Dots

As a stress specialist, I've watched stress levels climb in lockstep with the increased speed of society and the workplace.

The stress reaction is genetically encoded in us to create quick energy to fight or run away at times of danger—the classic fight-or-flight response. It was never intended to be turned on all the time. But when we're constantly fighting the clock and hurrying to keep up in a speeded-up world, our stress reactions are activated continuously. In addition to feeling pressed, over-loaded, and often overwhelmed, we experience serious biological effects as well.

When stress is ongoing, it impacts us physically, mentally, and emotionally. Here are some of the main effects:

- Increase in heart rate, blood pressure, and cholesterol, which predisposes us to cardiovascular disease, heart attacks, and strokes

- Insulin resistance, which can lead to weight gain, obesity, and eventually type 2 diabetes

- Suppression of the immune system, which increases risk of infections

- Muscle tension, which can be felt as headaches, neck and shoulder tightness, or lower-back pain and stiffness

- Fatigue and exhaustion (note that acute stress gives us increased energy but, if it goes on for too long, it becomes chronic stress and *drains* us of energy)

- Decrease in mental function, which affects concentration, memory, and decision making

- Mental health issues, especially anxiety, depression, and impatience

So, all this speed, hurrying, and rushing around is not only unpleasant but unhealthy. It affects how we feel and how we function. And it's unsustainable — at some point, our bodies start to fight back.

The first step in dealing with the problem is to recognize it. Patients are usually referred to me after they've hit the wall. One of my functions is to hold up a mirror and help them to see what's been going on. We all need to do this—as individuals, as organizations, and as a society.

The next step is to find solutions. More awareness leads to better choices.

CHAPTER 12

PRESCRIPTIONS AND SOLUTIONS

What can we do about this headlong rush we've gotten into, the ratcheted-up speed of our society? People are falling off the track at an alarming rate because they simply can't keep up. They're trying to be what they weren't designed or intended to be. And it's making them stressed and sick. What strategies will help us to take more control of our lives?

Face the Truth

Sam was referred to me with a long list of stress symptoms. He was a midlevel executive with a merchandising chain and was a self-described "driver," pushing himself hard to succeed and advance his career. When we calculated that he was working seventy hours a week, he wasn't all that surprised, but it had a powerful impact on him to see it on paper. Part of this was company-driven. He said, "The pace of my business is pretty intense. There's pressure to perform at a high level." But he admitted that much of it was self-imposed. He was trying to get ahead in a fiercely competitive world.

Sam finally decided to take action when he realized what it was costing him—anxiety, sleepless nights, preoccupation with work, lack of leisure time, and disconnection from his family. He started to make some changes; he cut back his work hours and was surprised at the result: "I'm understanding more about myself. I find I'm more productive working fewer hours."

Eventually he learned how to pace himself. "I understand how to slow down now. I need to spend more time being still." He became aware that "over time I allowed life, work, and other people to get into my soul. I'm not doing that as much anymore. I have to live my life with a little more moderation. I need to find a balance there." Along the way, Sam noted that "work isn't as important to me as it used to be." It was still important but no longer all-consuming. At a later visit, he said, "I'm not going back to the guy I used to be—the long hours. When I do that, I'm not productive, I'm not as happy, and I'm not as nice a guy to be around."

Develop Realistic Expectations

As I learned on the track in my youth, we can only go so fast. The real problem is unrealistic expectations. People can't keep accelerating *ad infinitum*. In terms of volume and hours of work, we have limits. As they say, you can only put eight ounces in an eight-ounce glass. Our jobs have become open-ended. Because of technology, we can now work anywhere and anytime. But we're limited by our physiology. We need a certain amount of sleep; we need to eat at regular intervals. Our brains can only concentrate for so long before

> Our jobs have become open-ended, but we're limited by our physiology.

our minds wander—research suggests that ninety minutes is the maximum for intense concentration.

We need to modify our expectations. A reality check would help. For example, many people defer tasks to the evening, such as writing reports, paying bills, doing their expense accounts, answering correspondence. They say, with the best of intentions, "I'll do this on Wednesday night." Then they get home from work, have supper, clean up the kitchen, and find they have no energy or motivation to do anything but veg out on the sofa. Or their spouse and kids want time with them. So they say, "I'll do it tomorrow night." But tomorrow never comes. If you keep planning to do things in the evening but find it never happens, stop pretending you can keep working at night and adjust your expectations to match reality.

Resist Tight Deadlines

The need for speed increases dramatically when we face numerous and tight deadlines. Deadlines are one of the most oppressive examples of artificial time running our lives. And *a lot* of them are arbitrary. They're set by the people with the power, sometimes managers and bosses, sometimes demanding clients. As the speed of life has accelerated, deadlines have gotten tighter. People want things ASAP and we've gotten into the habit of simply accepting these increasingly narrow timelines. Sadly, we work longer, harder, and faster to meet these compressed deadlines. The worst part is that every time we do this we convey the message that it's OK to keep doing this. And thus the treadmill (more aptly named the "dreadmill") continues to speed up.

As much as possible, and to the extent you have control over these issues at work, don't overpromise and underdeliver. Don't accept a deadline you can't meet confidently. Communicate your concerns and negotiate a time for completion that is comfortable and realistic. If you're unsure whether you can meet a deadline, accept the work only conditionally and express your reservation. If you see yourself running behind, let people know in advance.

Avoid "Last Minute-itis"

Dateline: April 30, 1975. The last day to file and pay income tax in Canada. A much younger David Posen leaves his office at 4:30 p.m. and rushes over to the post office with a manila envelope containing his tax return and cheque for the amount owing. He approaches the counter and asks the clerk to hand stamp the envelope showing that it was mailed before the 5 p.m. deadline. He then goes to the photocopier to make a copy of the envelope in case he has to prove that he mailed it on time. Then he drops the package in the bin, heaves a huge sigh of relief, and hustles back to his office to see the rest of his patients. On his way back, he swears he will never do this again—until he realizes he said the same thing last year when he left it to the last minute and did the same mad dash to the post office at the same wow-that-was-close hour.

There's nothing quite so stressful as that down-to-the-wire push to meet a deadline. Set some artificial timelines for yourself well ahead of the final completion date so you aren't frantically running and rushing at the eleventh hour.

Don't Overprogram or Overschedule Yourself

Type A people are notorious for trying to get more things done. They make long to-do lists, and then rush around trying to accomplish all the things on their list. It was called a "sense of time urgency" or "hurry sickness" by Drs. Meyer Friedman and Ray Rosenman in their book *Type A Behavior and Your Heart*. It's also a classic example of how volume drives velocity.

There's a trap in trying to do too much. When you have — or *feel* you have — a lot to do, you then feel you have to speed up to get it all done. You drive faster, you walk faster, you run to catch amber lights. Pretty soon, you're doing everything at an accelerated pace. There's a Zen saying that describes this: "How you do *anything* is how you do *everything.*"

Volume drives velocity.

A patient came to see me seeking help with time management. She wanted to know how to be more efficient so she could get more done. I asked her to read my first book, *Always Change a Losing Game*, before our next visit. When she came back, she said, "I realize I've been asking the wrong question. Instead of asking 'How can I do more?' I should be asking 'Why am I trying to do so *much?*'" With that insight, she cut back on the overtime she was putting in at work (most of it unpaid, not required, and taken for granted by her boss) and some other "shoulds" she'd imposed on herself — and made more time for herself and her children. By reducing the number of things she was trying to squeeze in, she was able to slow down the treadmill she'd created for herself. Not all of us have this option, given the pressures at work. But if you do, take it!

In addition to paring back some of our own overactivity, we should do the same for our children. Many kids are overprogrammed with after-school activities that keep them running from one thing to another, even in their "free time." Young children and teenagers need downtime, unstructured time to just hang out and play, to use their imaginations, to be with their friends. From ballet to soccer, drama to T-ball, Sunday school to piano, and Brownies to swimming, kids are not only overloaded now, they're learning to live at a pace that will not serve them well later in life.

Shorten Your To-Do Lists

Look at all the things you've got on the go now, both at work and in your home life. This includes projects, committees, home chores, errands, child care, elder care, hobbies, groups you belong to, volunteering, social media "friends" you're keeping in touch with, etc. Are there any items that are low value in terms of benefits and satisfaction? Is there anything that is no longer gratifying to you? Are there any "make-work" projects that are totally unnecessary? Pick one task, chore, or activity that you can let go of. Then spread the others out over the week, so you're not trying to do as much on any given day. If you're still overloaded or feeling pressured, pick something else to drop or at least to do less often. Do you really have to mow the lawn twice a week? How about once every five days? Keep adjusting until the pace of your life feels more comfortable to you.

Set Realistic Time Frames

It's fascinating how we underestimate the passing of time. How often have you been in a meeting or at lunch with a friend only to look at your watch and be shocked to find that it's much later than you thought? "I can't believe that hour went by so fast." "Have we really been here for two hours?"

Conversely, we often underestimate how long things actually take. How long do you think it takes to brush your teeth? Take a shower? Put on makeup? Eat your breakfast? (You *do* eat breakfast, don't you?) Not to make you a compulsive clock-watcher, but do a little experiment, check it out. Time yourself for a few days.

We do the same thing when travelling in our cars, getting our kids ready for school, making lunch, and doing tasks at work. If you think something takes thirty minutes but it really takes an hour, you will inevitably fall behind. Then you will start rushing to catch up. If you're always fighting the clock and running late, start to leave realistic time frames for your activities and you'll eliminate the huffing-and-puffing factor from your life.

How about bigger projects such as writing a report or decluttering your home? There was an article in the *Canadian Medical Association Journal* aimed at doctors who thought they'd like to write a book. Mostly tongue in cheek, it cited the "first law of authorship (Bumm's Law) which states that the work required to complete any given book is precisely 7.16 times the amount of work the author thought would be required and 3.92 times the maximum amount of time available to devote to it." Many things take longer than you think.

Leave Buffer Time

Even after you schedule realistic time frames for your activities, unexpected things will often come up. The other morning I rode the commuter train into Toronto. There was a medical emergency on board and the train arrived ten minutes late. I then took the subway to my meeting and, believe it or not, there was a delay on that train too — also because of a medical emergency; as they say, "Stuff happens!"

Protect yourself against the buffeting effect of such events by leaving a bit of extra time as a cushion. If it takes twenty minutes to get to the airport, leave thirty minutes for the trip. If you need a half hour to shower and dress for work, give yourself a little extra.

Stop Squeezing in "One More Thing"

Are you one of those people who hate to waste time? Do you squeeze short tasks or activities into any little crack or smidgeon of time that presents itself? No downtime for these folks! For example, they plan to leave for a meeting at 1:30. They're ready at 1:25. No sense "wasting" five minutes. They return a phone call or fire off an email. Then they can't find their keys or someone asks them a question just as they're leaving. Now they're running late and having to hurry.

If this sounds familiar, avoid the temptation to shoehorn "one more thing" into every bit of daylight in your schedule. Treat yourself to that extra five minutes for a more relaxed trip to the meeting or for the opportunity, when you arrive, to chat with a colleague or glance at a magazine.

Find a Pace That's Comfortable for You

As a family physician, I used to see about twenty to twenty-five patients a day in my office. This was in addition to making rounds at the hospital, assisting in the OR, dealing with emergencies, delivering babies, making house calls, and my *favourite* activity, doing the paperwork! My patient visits included longer appointments for two complete physical examinations and at least two talk sessions (psychotherapy) each day. A busy day was thirty to thirty-five patients, and forty felt really hectic. I enjoyed taking time with my patients and being thorough in my work. But I had colleagues who could see fifty patients in an afternoon. Some even bragged of seeing seventy-five to one hundred a day! I can't imagine practising medicine that way, but that's beside the point. The good news about being a self-employed solo practitioner was that I had the freedom to set my own pace. It was busy and stressful, but quite manageable.

Most people don't have the luxury of setting their own pace at work. If you're self-employed, find a rhythm and routine that feels comfortable for you. Find ways to slow things down a little. If you work for someone else, do your best to manage your workload so you're not feeling rushed all the time. Talk to your boss and coworkers. If you're a manager or supervisor, be aware that everyone who reports to you has a different comfort zone for speed and efficiency. Push them beyond that and you'll get diminishing returns from their effort. Enlightened managers understand this and don't overload or push their people too hard. They tailor the work to each individual's capability and capacity.

In your nonwork life, the same principle applies. Find and establish a pace that feels good for you. Slow down, even just a little. I ask my type A patients to ratchet back just 5 to 10 percent.

(Anything more than that and they'd feel like they were living in slow motion!) Life is to be lived, not raced through. Stop fighting the clock in your leisure and family time. Enjoy some open-ended, relaxing activities (for example, hanging out with friends, doing a jigsaw puzzle, or hiking in the country).

Stop Clock-Watching on Weekends

Take off your watch if you wear one. Let yourself settle into a slower, more natural rhythm. Better yet, go out into nature for a hike or sit by a lake and feel what it's like to have no agenda, no place you have to be and no timeline for a few hours.

Decide What's Important to You — and Make Time for It

Other than my work and time with my family, there are things that I bring into my life on a regular basis. One is daily exercise. I walk, ride my bike, or play a sport every day. I rarely miss because it's important to my health—and very enjoyable. I eat three meals a day and get eight hours of sleep most nights. I meditate several times a week.

So much for the virtuous stuff. One of my great pleasures is doing the weekend crossword puzzles in the newspaper. Reading is a passion for me, both fiction and non-fiction, and I read every day, even if only at bedtime. Since we became empty nesters several years ago, I have more time for music and play trombone in a wind

"The key is not to prioritize your schedule but to schedule your priorities."
— Stephen Covey

orchestra. My wife and I play Scrabble regularly, go to movies, and socialize with friends. I also keep in touch with family and friends by phone.

When our children were younger, I had less discretionary time, but I still did many of the things I've listed above. What are the important things in *your* life? Are you making time for them now? If not, pick one item and figure out when you will do it. It might be a daily activity, like eating breakfast, or something done less often such as a hobby or meeting a friend for lunch. Just start somewhere! Start making time for the things you value and enjoy. So many lives are filled with "have to dos" and include far too few "want to dos."

Add a Few Words to Your Vocabulary

As mentioned earlier, Anthony Newley and Leslie Bricusse wrote a marvellous musical called *Stop the World — I Want to Get Off.* If only it were that simple. Although some people *do* get out of the rat race and open up a bed-and-breakfast in Nova Scotia, most people will continue to live in urban areas where life moves faster than many of them would like. But that doesn't mean they have to be total victims.

It's pushback time. If you work or live with people who are trying to hurry you up, it's time to take a stand and advocate for yourself. We can all speed up at times, when required. But as a way of life, trying to run faster than your own comfort level makes no sense. It's unpleasant, very stressful, and unsustainable. Especially when people are pushing you for *their own* benefit, you have to speak up. Some simple words to add to your vocabulary include "enough" and "no." "Boundaries" and "limits" are other words to keep in mind. This isn't about being difficult or rebellious; it's not about being a poor team player or uncooperative. It's about taking care of yourself, your needs, and your health. If people make unreasonable or unrealistic demands and you comply, what are you telling them? You're basically saying, "It's OK to treat me this way." You're giving them tacit permission to keep pushing or even exploiting you. And if you deliver that silent message, nothing will change. (Note: I acknowledge that it might not be easy to say "no" or "enough" on your own, especially at work. But if you get like-minded people to join you, it's possible to do so collectively.)

> Being selective is self-protective.

Another word to think of is "tilt." If you start pushing a pinball machine around too much, a light with the word "TILT" goes on and the machine shuts down. It's basically saying, "You can't do this to me anymore." We need to learn to say "tilt" in our own lives when we're being pushed beyond our point of tolerance or comfort—especially if *we're* the ones pushing *ourselves*.

Avoid Multitasking

Vince Poscente's *The Age of Speed* caught my eye in a bookstore. I bought it out of curiosity because I disagreed with its premise that "harnessing the power of speed is the ultimate solution for those seeking less stress, less busyness, and more balance." As I paid for the book, I thought to myself, *OK, Vince. Convince me!* By page eight he had me, assuaging my cynicism by explaining that speed "helps people spend less time doing meaningless things to make room for more significant living." In other words, if we can do the mundane things in life more quickly, we'll free up more time for relaxation, relationships, hobbies, fun, and exciting activities.

In showing how speed can be used advantageously, Poscente also identifies three things that slow us down (especially in the workplace) and thus decrease our efficiency and lengthen our work hours. One is interruptions, such as phone calls or people dropping by. The second is email. The third is multitasking.

Let's look at this third item. A lot of people think that multitasking is a great way to increase productivity. After all, if you always do two things at once, you can get twice as much done, right? Well, actually, *wrong!* We're built to focus, not to split-screen. Research shows quite clearly that multitasking reduces efficiency and productivity by up to 50 percent. You miss things. You lose time. And you make mistakes. Sometimes more is *less!* The solution? Mono- or single-tasking, doing one thing at a time — sequentially. This will both improve your productivity and reduce your stress.

Pick Your Lane

Every time we get on a highway, we decide which lane we want to travel in. "Sunday drivers" and relaxed folks stay to the right. Motorists wanting a zippier trip choose the middle lane. The left lane is supposed to be the passing lane, but folks in a real hurry usually make a beeline for it and then just stay there for the whole trip. (If you want to start a local chapter of certified type As, just grab the licence plate numbers of all the left lane cars and you'll have your membership filled in no time.)

As with highway driving, we can all pick the lane we want to travel through life in. Watch people walking on Bloor Street in Toronto or Fifth Avenue in New York City and you'll see individuals voting with their feet on the pace they want to follow. Some amble, some walk more quickly, and some speed-walk as if they're about to break into a run at any moment. My mother was a fast walker. I remember how hard it was to keep up with her when I was a kid. I can't imagine what it would have been like to have to do that for a lifetime. "Effortful," "breathless," and "relentless" are words that come to mind. And no time to pause and look around.

In today's hyperaccelerated world, the pace is being set by the swiftest. It's as though a few gifted people can run a four-minute mile so now we're all expected to run that fast. Somehow we feel we have to speed up in order to keep up. But we really don't. We aren't compelled to conform to a pace that's unpleasant and unsustainable for us. We can each choose how fast we'd like to go.

Pick Your Rhythm: Speeding Up and Slowing Down

Did you know that "if you set two out-of-sync pendulum clocks side by side, by the next day they will be keeping time together"? So notes Stephan Rechtschaffen in his book *Time Shifting*. He adds: "It looks as if they *want* to be locked into sync with each other." Go for a walk with someone and notice how soon your footfalls become co-ordinated with no conscious attention or effort. You fall into a rhythmic pace with each other.

Everything in nature moves in rhythm. The movement of the sun, the moon, the stars, and the tides all reflect this. In our own bodies there are two obvious examples of rhythmicity: our heartbeats and our breathing. Whether your heart beats fast or slow, there is a regular rhythm. The average person breathes twelve to fourteen times a minute. The rate may speed up or slow down, depending on your activity level or emotional state, but it still has a regular rhythm. In fact, it's a very accurate indication of our internal state, both physical and emotional.

As humans, we absorb the rhythms around us. Rechtschaffen calls it "entrainment." Have you ever noticed how an excitable person can set off a speeded-up feeling inside you? You start to feel a bit hyper around hyper people. Similarly, someone who talks in a slow, soothing voice can have a calming effect on you.

It seems that music is the most effective entrainer. Think of a school dance or the proms of your youth. To get people into a party mood, they played a lot of fast songs to get everyone hopping. Periodically, there would be a slow number to give people a breather. But for the last dance, they always played some slow, dreamy song and dimmed the lights to create a mood of romance and intimacy. At funerals, slow and quiet music creates an appropriately sombre mood. At rock concerts, people often jump up and start dancing to the beat. Music is in our bodies and in our very souls.

Here's the interesting part: we can be swept along by whatever music we're exposed to — or we can *choose* the music we want to listen to. When I drive to a venue to give a speech, I often listen to classical music to put me in a relaxed mood. On my way home, and especially when the speech has gone well and it's a beautiful sunny day, I'll open my sun roof, put on some rock 'n' roll, crank up the volume, and groove to the energy and excitement of the music. I choose music to either suit my mood or to *create* a mood.

Entrainment is neither good nor bad. It just *is*. It's a natural phenomenon. Once I started to notice it and to be more aware of how it was affecting me, I began making different choices in my life. When I was younger, I was a fast-paced, rushing-around, type A poster boy. I still like fast and exciting events at times, but I pick and choose more carefully now.

Our lives should be like a symphony. In orchestral music, there are fast passages and slow passages. It's the variety that makes the music interesting. But there are also rests in music, pauses between the notes. These moments of silence are very powerful. We need them in our lives as well. I allow my life to get busy or even hectic at times. In manageable amounts, it makes things dynamic and exciting. But I do so only for limited periods before I build in a break to slow down and get quiet.

We're living in a world that has speeded up dramatically. As Rechtschaffen notes, "Unconsciously we have entrained with a faster rhythm. It controls the way we walk, the way we speak, the way we respond to intimates and strangers, the way we *don't* relax. This habituation to simply skim the surface of experiences then move on, it permeates our lives. Modern society's rhythm provides perhaps the most powerful and — potentially the most pernicious — entrainment of all."

The good news is that we can shift our rhythms. We're not stuck with one pace. Nor are we condemned to fall into line with the ambient frantic rhythms around us. We don't have to conform to society's rhythms all the time. We can step off the hamster wheel, at least temporarily. We have choices — not all the time, but more often than we may acknowledge. We don't have to be fighting the clock at every turn. Just remember: *many things in your life are there because you put them there.* The length of your to-do list, the speed you've adopted in your life, the commitments you accept, and the promises you make are all potentially within the realm of your control. If they're not serving you well, you can change them.

More awareness leads to better choices.

CHAPTER 13

IS IT TOO LATE TO TURN BACK THE CLOCK? (PUN INTENDED)

Can we turn back the clock on our frenetic, frazzled culture? Absolutely! Not only *can* we address this issue, but there will be increasingly harsh consequences if we don't. The good news is that we don't have to reverse everything nor do we have to do a complete 180 and go back to where we were. We just need to modify the things that have gone too far or gotten out of control. We can do this either individually or collectively. All we need is the will to do it.

People vote with their feet all the time. They leave workaholic, pressure-cooker workplaces for companies that are less driven and more balanced. Sometimes they start their own enterprises where they can set the tone and the pace. Two lawyers were tired of the rat race of working long days to chase billable hours and left the profession to start their own public education company, which has been a huge success. One young man left a high-speed treadmill job for a healthier-paced position with a company that wasn't trying to wear people out. Two young PR professionals in a high-powered ad agency got fed up with the intense pressure, constant deadlines, and brutal hours, and decided to get out of the whirlwind. They started their own advertising firm with a small staff, civilized hours, and a comfortable pace while still working in a field they loved and were good at. In recent years, many promising employees have turned down promotions because they don't want the hassle, pressure, and long hours. Many of my patients have negotiated more compatible working arrangements with their employers, asking only to be judged on performance and results, not speed, face time, or long hours. They've modified their hours, worked some days from home, and slowed the pace enough for them to function more effectively.

Think of what might be possible if we, as a society, decided that our frantic lifestyle of fast pace, long hours, fast food, crushing deadlines, and fragmented family life is harmful to health and well-being. People — and societies — need to be self-correcting. It would be the height of stubbornness and hubris to think we never make mistakes or go down the wrong road at times. That kind of arrogance leads to disaster. Human progress has never been a straight line forward and upward. Not only are we *capable* of self-reflection and change, our lives *depend* on it. The place to start is with each individual, then with families and small groups — and ultimately, as communities, towns, cities, etc.

We're living faster than nature and our biology intended. When every day feels like a race against time, life gets awfully stressful — and exhausting! We're pushing ourselves not only beyond our level of comfort, but in many cases, beyond our level of *tolerance*. And it's costing us — as individuals and as a society.

To be sure, it's not a problem for everyone. Some people love speed; they thrive on it. They're bored or frustrated without it. But for others, speed is unpleasant and unhealthy. There is no one size that fits all. We all have to make choices.

Nor is it all or nothing. We can all speed up at times. It can even be fun and exciting to do so. We can — and should — leave our comfort zones for short periods. We can even learn to expand our comfort zones. But there are limits for all of us.

Can We Slow Down as a Society?

Can we reverse this race we've gotten into? I believe we can. It's already happening, one person at a time, with folks making different and healthier choices. I see it in my practice on a regular basis. One of my patients said, "I'm slowing the pace and getting more done." I asked him if he felt better or restless when he slowed down. He replied, "If I'm camping, I can slow down. It's one of the great relaxing experiences in my life. It feels right when I slow down. It's *me!*" Interestingly, his frame of reference for slowing down was when he was camping, when he returned to nature and the slower rhythms that life was about for thousands of years. He went on to say, "I used to ask myself, many times a day, 'What is wrong with me? Why am I feeling so lousy? This isn't what life should be about.' Now I say, 'Ahh, this is more like it.'" Here is a man who returned to living in sync with himself, living in a rhythm that was congruent with his authentic, natural self. This is what's possible for most of us. In some cases it might require a major shift. But for many people, even ratcheting back a little will yield significant benefits.

It's also happening in small groups of like-minded people who decide to get off the roller-coaster and try the Ferris wheel instead. The professionals who leave big firms to go out on their own and set a more humane pace. The work teams who agree to set limits on their smartphone use or not use them at all. The families who off-load some of their extracurricular activities to spend more unstructured time together at home, relaxing. The people who move out of cities to the slower pace of small towns. We can choose our own pace—or at least decide how much of the fast-moving world we want to buy into.

To each his own. For people who want to live in the fast lane, have at it. For those who aspire to a dynamic, exciting life, go for it. For those who want to be workaholics and driven type As, help yourself. Just don't push, cajole, or bully others who aren't so inclined. Don't expect or require them to have the same desires you do. This applies to employers, coworkers, teachers, coaches, spouses, and parents. Do what you want in your own life (work and nonwork), but don't run your racket on other people.

As a society, we stopped seeing heavy drinkers as good ol' boys, we stopped viewing smokers as suave and cool, and we stopped looking at obesity as a sign of affluence. The day will come, sooner than later, when workaholism will be seen as aberrant and sad, not as a badge of honour; when long hours will be seen as shortsighted and unproductive; when constantly being hurried and rushed will announce, "Look at how inefficient and disorganized I am!"; when choosing to work sixty to seventy hours a week will be interpreted as, "Hey, look, I have no life!"; when not taking vacations will be seen as silly and strange, rather than conveying, "Look how important and indispensable I am." Societal values change. We'll all be the better for slowing down this runaway train we're on.

It's time to reclaim your life and to live more in sync with yourself. If *you* don't take control of your life, someone else will.

SECTION 3

THE SLEEP YOU NEED
VS.
THE SLEEP YOU GET

CHAPTER 14

SLEEP DEPRIVATION: UNDERESTIMATED AND MISUNDERSTOOD

There are two ways for a schoolteacher to ask a question. The first is to name a student and then ask the question — "Susan, what is the capital of Bolivia?" The second is to ask the question and then name the pupil you want to answer it: "What is the capital of Bolivia... John?" My grade eleven English teacher often chose the latter method as a way of exposing students who were half-asleep in class. She would ask the question, then scan the room for the student with the heaviest eyelids or one who was clearly asleep. Then she would pounce. She enjoyed watching teenagers either groggily come out of their stupor or, more often, sit bolt upright with eyes wide at the mention of their name. She then had the pleasure of observing the stressed individuals fumble to try to pluck the question from their hazy memory banks and come up with some credible reply.

Several possible outcomes ensued from this scenario. If the student floundered and couldn't remember the question, or didn't know the answer, our teacher had a look of smug satisfaction. If the student was flustered and embarrassed, it was a double win. If the student could actually remember the question and answer correctly, there was an unmistakable look of disappointment on the teacher's face. If a classmate nearby whispered the question — and even better, the answer — the student would have a look of relief on his face and, again, the teacher would be perturbed that her ruse had failed.

The story of high school students being half-asleep for half the morning is not new. But in our hurry-up culture of over-work, long commutes, and twenty-four-hour digital media, sleep deprivation doesn't only affect teenagers; it is widespread across society and the cost is staggering.

The tyranny of time and lack of sleep are two of the defining issues of our modern age. They're interconnected and both have serious implications for stress and ill health.

As a physician, I have always been interested in the health habits of my patients, focusing on nutrition, exercise, caffeine and alcohol consumption, and sleep. All of those issues are important, but in recent years I've paid increasing attention to sleep, struck by how sleep deprived most of my stressed-out patients are, and the effect it has on their health, both physical and mental. That is why this section is devoted specifically to sleep — and to the gap between the sleep we *need* and the sleep we *get*. This view was reinforced for me by Dr. Matthew Walker, neuroscience and psychology professor at University of California Berkeley. In a recent *Time* magazine article on longevity, Walker wrote, "I used to suggest that sleep is the third pillar of good health, along with diet and exercise. But I don't agree with that anymore. Sleep is the single most effective thing you can do to reset your brain and body for health."

> "Sleep is the single most effective thing you can do to reset your brain and body for health."
> — Dr. Matthew Walker

How Big is the Disconnect between What You Need and What You Get?

Dr. Stanley Coren is a psychologist at the University of British Columbia in Vancouver. Many people know him as a dog expert, but he also wrote a wonderful book called *Sleep Thieves*. I had the privilege of speaking with Dr. Coren many years ago and he told me an interesting story about writing the book. He said that he was not a sleep specialist but was actually studying differences of various kinds. (He'd already written a book about left-handedness called *The Left Hander Syndrome*.) Coren said he took a group of self-declared "short sleepers," people who said that they only slept five hours a night, that that was all they needed, and that they functioned quite well. He put them in sleep labs and took away all their time cues. They had no clocks, watches, windows, phones, radios or TVs—no way to reckon what time it was. They all slept nine hours.

Some people might be forgiven for not realizing how much sleep they actually require to function well. But there's a more perplexing problem in our society: many people *know* how much sleep they need and still don't *get* it.

Grab a pencil and write down the number of hours of sleep you think you need to function at your best. Not what you can get away with, but what you *need* to feel the best that you can feel and to function optimally. Then write down "yes" if you actually *get* that number most nights (not necessarily *every* night, but *most* nights.) Write "no" if you *don't* get that number of hours of sleep on a regular basis. I do this exercise in many of my seminars and invariably more than half the people in the group write "no." Most people are not getting the number of hours sleep that they themselves say they need.

Now, if you wrote "no" to the previous question, write down how much *less* sleep you're getting than what you said you *need*. For example, if you need eight hours and you get seven, you have a shortfall of one hour. It's called a "sleep debt." I'm shocked to see how many people have a sleep debt of two or more hours each night. I will elaborate further on this in chapter 17, but suffice it to say that even *an hour* less per night on a regular basis will have serious consequences.

> "I consider the pervasive lack of awareness about sleep deprivation a national emergency."
> — Dr. William Dement

We're a sleep-deprived society. Statistics pop up everywhere you look. A Gallup poll in 2013 found that Americans averaged 6.8 hours of sleep a night, down more than an hour from 1942 and down *two hours* from a century ago. In 2011, Statistics Canada found that 30 percent of Canadians got less than 6 hours sleep per night. A 2017 National Sleep Foundation poll found weekday sleep numbers were similar: 29 percent of people got less than 6 hours a night, 41.3 percent got 6 to 7 hours, 21.5 percent got 7 to 8 hours, and 8.2 percent got more than 8 hours.

Here are two pieces of evidence to make the point, one objective and the other subjective. The first was a study by Dr. Coren, exploring how sleep deprived Canadians are by looking at negative consequences. He came up with a clever idea. Coren looked at what happens when everyone in Canada loses an hour of sleep in the same night. That occurs in the spring when we switch to daylight savings time. (There is one exception in Canada: the province of Saskatchewan does not change its clocks. The state of Arizona also maintains standard time year-round.) He then looked at the motor vehicle accident rate the day after the time change. The results were very clear. On the Monday following the time change, the motor-vehicle-accident rate rose by 7 percent. The results were replicated in each province, two years in a row. He then mused on what happens in the fall when we turn our clocks back and *gain* an hour. Lo and behold, the motor-vehicle-accident rate on the Monday after the time change *fell by 7 percent!* Again, this was replicated two years in a row. Coren concluded that if one hour of sleep gained or lost in only one night can make such a statistically significant difference, we must be pretty sleep deprived as a society. We must be right on the razor's edge so that one hour either way can tip us that much.

The second piece of evidence is subjective and a little playful. It comes from an Ipsos-Reid study on free time done several years ago. One of the questions was, "If you had a choice between a good night of sleep and a good night of sex, which would you prefer?" The results amused a lot of people: 58 percent of Canadians said they would prefer a good night of sleep, and 37 percent said they would prefer a good night of sex. If you add up those two numbers, it comes to 95 percent. I've always wondered what the other 5 percent were doing when they were asked the question!

"The research about sleep deprivation is now as compelling as that of the dangers of smoking fifty years ago." — Dr. Charles Czeisler, head of the Sleep Medicine division at Harvard Medical School

When I share these statistics in my seminars, a lot of men say, "Ah, come on, *guys* wouldn't say that." And it's true there was a gender difference: 44 percent of men said they would prefer a good night's sleep, but 72 percent of women said they would prefer a good night of sleep. (Incidentally, this does not surprise most women.) In any case, when people prefer sleep over sex you know that something is wrong. We're a sleep-deprived society craving sleep and yet most of us still aren't getting enough.

CHAPTER 15

HOW DO YOU KNOW HOW MUCH SLEEP YOU NEED AND WHETHER YOU'RE GETTING ENOUGH?

As part of my lifestyle assessment with patients, I always ask how much sleep they get in an average night. It's usually six or seven hours. Then I ask them how much they *need* to function at their best, to feel terrific (not just what they can get away with, because we can all get away with less). About 90 percent give me a number immediately—and the number is usually around eight hours. You don't have to be Sherlock Holmes to figure out what the problem is here. Very few of these people are actually getting the amount of sleep they themselves say they need.

Most people have a sense of the number of hours of sleep they need to function optimally. The research tells us it's between 7.5 and 8.5 hours a night. The most exacting studies apparently narrow it down to eight hours and fifteen minutes. A general rule is that we need one hour of sleep for every two hours awake. So every twenty-four hours, we have sixteen hours awake and need eight hours of sleep. However, it's a range. A lucky few truly need only six hours a night, but there are far fewer than you may think. According to the journal *Science*, about 3 percent of the population have a genetic mutation that results in them needing only six hours of sleep a night. In *The Sleep Revolution*, Arianna Huffington puts that figure at 1 percent. The other 97 to 99

> The general guideline is one hour of sleep for every two hours awake. So for every twenty-four-hour cycle, we need eight hours of sleep for every sixteen hours awake.

percent of us need more. There's generally a range from seven to nine hours a night with a lucky few needing only six, and a few requiring ten. But it's a bell curve with small numbers at both low and high ends and most of us in the middle.

I use five criteria when evaluating if people are getting the sleep they need.

1. Do you need an alarm to wake you up every morning? If so, you're probably sleep deprived.

2. Do you wake up feeling rested and refreshed or tired and groggy? If you keep hitting the snooze button and wishing that you could stay in bed, you're not getting enough sleep.

3. How's your daytime energy? Do you struggle through the day? Do you get tired easily? Do you get sleepy when reading technical material or when sitting in meetings or dark rooms? Do you start fading on your drive home from work? Do you flake out on the sofa after supper and often fall asleep? If so, you're not getting the sleep you need.

4. How long do you sleep when you don't have to wake up? For example, do you sleep longer on weekends or on vacation? If so, you're probably making up some of the sleep debt that you've built up.

5. How long does it take you to fall asleep at night? Called the "sleep latency period," this is the criterion used by sleep researchers to assess how sleep deprived you are. If you fall asleep within five or ten minutes (or less), you may think that means that you're a great sleeper. But in fact it means

you're sleep deprived. Fully rested people actually take about fifteen minutes to fall asleep naturally. If you fall asleep quickly, it's because your brain is so sleep starved that it shuts down as fast as possible. So if you brag, as I did for years, about how fast you can fall asleep, or that you can fall asleep anywhere, what you're really saying is, "Hey, look at me. I'm sleep deprived!"

What Do the Experts Say?

There is some variability in individual sleep requirements so there's no absolute number for everyone. However, on average, the guidelines look something like this:

SLEEP REQUIREMENTS (BY AGE)	
Birth to age 1	16–18 hours/day (although not all at once)
12–24 months	14–15 hours/day (including naps)
2–5 years	12 hours/day
Age 5 to puberty	10 hours/day
Teenagers	9–10 hours/night
Adults	7–9 hours/night

One myth to debunk: we don't need less sleep as we get to old age. However much sleep you need in your thirties and forties is what you need in your seventies and eighties — possibly a bit less. It's just that for many ageing citizens, it's harder to *get* that amount of sleep for a multitude of health reasons, so they often sleep less.

Teenagers and Sleep

To say that teens are different than adults is to state the obvious. Growth spurts, body changes, identity crises, the onset of conceptual thinking, raging hormones, distinctive fashion styles and music, a sudden interest in sex, shifting focus from their heroic parents to their all-important peer group—it's all part of the territory. But there's another important change that affects teens. It's called "phase shift delay." As Mary Carskadon of Brown University puts it, "Body clocks reset themselves around puberty, making the natural sleep time about an hour later." Now, teenagers still need a lot of sleep—at least nine hours a night and often ten or eleven. Good luck finding a teen who gets that much! Most get less than eight hours in an average night. Being an adolescent is hard enough without being chronically starved for sleep.

For whatever reason—nature operates in mysterious ways— the teen brain doesn't shut down until around 11 p.m., delaying the fall in cortisol and secretion of melatonin that heralds the natural onset of slumber. Correspondingly, their brains don't wake up until later in the morning. The result is that they're out of sync with the world around them for the better part of ten years.

This disharmony shows up most dramatically at school. Edina, Minnesota, was the first school district in the U.S. to recognize and address the problem. In 1996, they moved the start time of classes from 7:20 a.m. to 8:30 a.m. Even though the change was modest, the results were significant. Students were more alert and less depressed. The changes were so significant that thirty-four districts in nineteen states had followed Edina's lead by 2003. But even though there are multiple benefits from this policy, only 14.4 percent of U.S. high schools start classes at 8:30 a.m. or later. Studies of later-starting schools show a reduction in lateness, sleeping in class, car accidents, substance abuse, and depression. They also report improved attendance, graduation rates, and standardized-test scores.

A colleague told me a related story from Montreal in the 1970s. Because of overcrowding, one school district had to divide high school classes into morning and afternoon groups. The early-morning cohort was schooled from about 7:30 a.m. until noon. The afternoon students went from 12:30 to 5 p.m. An unin- tended consequence was that the afternoon class outperformed the morning group so dramatically that the parents of the early pupils insisted that the groups be reversed for the second semes- ter. Students whose school schedule matched their biological clocks and sleep cycles did better academically and had fewer behaviour problems. Why they didn't shift all the students to a later start time after that is a question that mystifies me. It's time to make that standard practice. Optimally, I'd like to see high school classes go from 10 a.m. to 4 p.m.

Phase Shift Advance in the Elderly

There's a great scene in the movie *City Slickers* in which Billy Crystal's character visits his kid's elementary school class on career day to talk about his job as an accountant. Instead, he has a meltdown and starts talking about how fast life flies by. He goes through the decades and lists the things that happen to people: "In your seventies, you eat dinner at two o'clock in the afternoon, lunch around ten, and breakfast the night before." He could have added that you start going to bed and waking up earlier too. Many folks in their eighties and nineties are tucked in by 9 p.m. and up with the chirping birds at five in the morning. Just as teens have a phase shift delay, older adults experience a phase shift *advance*. Their normal wakeup and shutdown times are earlier by an hour or two. Again, this is physiological and hard-wired.

CHAPTER 16

WHY WE SLEEP AND THE COST OF SLEEP DEPRIVATION

A lot of people want to resist nature. I bought a book purporting to explain how we can train our bodies to need less sleep. *Terrific*, I thought. *I'm up for that. Less sleep means more time for reading, sports, music, family, and friends. What could be bad?* And indeed the book began with all the benefits we'd experience if we needed less sleep. There's only one problem: it doesn't work. Sleep-wise, we need what we need — and when we shortchange ourselves, we pay a price.

So many folks view sleep as expendable or even frivolous, something that's only for wimps. They say things like "sleep is such a waste of time" or "I'll get all the sleep I need when I'm dead." But sleep is crucial to our health and well-being. It's a time for renewal and repair. Sleep is like a minihibernation: heart rate slows, blood pressure and body temperature fall, metabolic rate slows down. It's when we replenish our energy. It's when we fight off infection. It's when hormones promoting growth and cell and tissue repair are secreted. Sleep is a time for rest, recovery, and healing.

Paradoxically, while the body is in a resting state, the brain is surprisingly active. It's like rebooting a computer to get everything aligned and humming again. This is when we do our "mental housekeeping." The brain is processing all the experiences of the previous day, reinforcing and consolidating memory tracks, and also getting rid of irrelevant information and unimportant memories that can clog up the neuronal circuits and create too much background noise. Many sleep scientists believe that a primary function of sleep is to clean out the brain of debris and metabolic waste that accumulates during the day. Brain cells (neurons) actually contract during sleep, creating spaces between them so that fluid can wash out dangerous toxins that can damage or interfere with efficient brain function.

So, why is this information important and why should you care? What is the cost of this lack of sleep? The answer is huge and significant.

Sleep Deprivation Presents in Several Ways:

1. **We feel physically tired.**
   Fatigue is the most common complaint patients bring to their family doctor. It's also one of the early symptoms of chronic stress. But it's nonspecific. It can result from a number of causes. The most obvious is not getting enough sleep.

2. **Our mental functions are affected.**
   This can include a decrease in concentration and short-term memory, and slower decision making. The next time you think of pulling an all-nighter — to cram for exams or to finish a report for work — you might want to reconsider your decision. Functional MRIs monitor brain function in real time, showing which parts of the brain are active during any mental activity. They do this by showing where the blood flow is greatest at any given second. I have a slide showing functional MRI images of two people doing arithmetic tasks. One subject is fully rested. That person's MRI shows multiple areas of activity reflected by yellow and red colours in various

places. The second subject had been awake for thirty-five hours. You'd be hard-pressed to find any activity at all. It's like someone's home, but the lights are all off!

Dr. Stanley Coren notes that we lose one point of IQ when we lose one hour of sleep in a given night (from the required eight.) But, for every *additional* hour lost, we lose *two* points. And it's cumulative.

> Being awake is not the same as being alert.

So if you're one of the multitude of people with a sleep debt of two hours a night, you lose three IQ points every night. By the end of the workweek, you've lost *fifteen points*. If you take the average IQ of 100 points dropping to 85, you're talking about serious mental impairment. But, as Dr. Coren notes, even for people with a higher IQ rating of 115 dropping to 100, your short-term memory goes along with flexible thinking. You talk in clichés, and you struggle to hold on to complex ideas in your head or act on them sensibly. Your brain goes on autopilot.

In his book *The 20-Minute Break*, Dr. Ernest Rossi reveals how sleep deprivation affects labour negotiations and is sometimes used purposely by mediators to break down resistance between parties in order to secure a deal. As one government mediator put it, "Some pretty dumb things begin to sound logical when you've been negotiating all night and it's now 5 a.m."

3. Our mood is affected.

We become more irritable, more easily frustrated, quicker to anger, and even depressed. These mood changes affect our relationships, both at work and at home. Tired people are cranky, grumpy, and not a lot of fun to be around.

4. **Our resistance to infection is lowered.**
   This is because our immune system is most active when we sleep. This is when we produce T-lymphocytes, which are the killer white blood cells that destroy bacteria and viruses. This is why, when people get sick, they often say, "I got run-down so I came down with the flu." The fact is that lack of sleep directly affects our ability to resist infection.

Here's a little zinger about the above list. These are not only symptoms of sleep deprivation, but also symptoms of *stress*. Sleep deprivation actually shows up in our bodies as stress. It gets worse. Lack of sleep raises levels of cortisol, the main hormone in chronic stress. It gets even worse than *that*. When we're sleep deprived, we're less resilient in dealing with stressful situations. We're more likely to overreact to things or take offence at other people's behaviour. And if *that's* not bad enough, stress itself can lead to insomnia and further loss of sleep, thus creating a vicious cycle.

> "Whoever we are, wherever we are in our lives, sleep is the ultimate performance enhancer, with no nasty side effects."
> —Arianna Huffington

Lack of Sleep Can Make You Fat

Here's another piece of joyful news. One of the functions of sleep is to regulate hormone production. One of the hormones secreted during sleep controls appetite. It's called leptin and it's secreted by fat cells. It controls feelings of hunger and appetite just as a thermostat controls temperature. It's sometimes referred to as our "appestat." When you're fully rested, leptin puts the brakes on your food intake. It tells you when you've had enough to eat, when you're satiated or "full." When you're sleep deprived, leptin levels fall and your internal monitoring system is thrown off. You feel hungry even when you've had enough to eat—especially craving carbohydrates, sweets, and high-fat foods. So you overeat and put on weight.

To add to the problem, ghrelin is another hormone affecting weight. It's a peptide; produced mainly in the stomach, it works by stimulating appetite. Lack of sleep *increases* ghrelin levels, thus increasing our desire for food. So, along with the appetite-suppressing hormone leptin *decreasing* with insufficient sleep, these are two effects of sleep deprivation that increase eating and lead to weight gain. Being overweight can lead to obesity, which in turn can predispose you to heart disease, type 2 diabetes, osteoarthritis, and other health problems. Not a happy spiral to get into.

Russell Sanna, executive director of Harvard's Division of Sleep Medicine, sums it up neatly: Without adequate sleep, "you get sick, fat, and stupid." To which I'd add the word "sad" because there's a definite link between sleep deprivation and mood—especially depression.

> Without adequate sleep, "you get sick, fat, and stupid."

Lack of Sleep Can Affect Your Judgement

As Steve Jobs famously used to say, "Oh, there's one more thing." When we're tired, we don't realize how impaired we are, so we think we're functioning normally when we're not. This is especially dangerous when it leads to lowered vigilance or denial. Sleepy drivers are the classic example.

Statistics suggest that 60 percent of Americans have driven while sleepy, while 30 percent of Americans have fallen asleep at the wheel within the past year. In *The Sleep Revolution*, Arianna Huffington cites a 2014 study by the AAA Foundation for Traffic Safety that showed drowsy drivers in the U.S. are involved in 328,000 accidents each year, with 6,400 resulting in fatalities. Not only is judgement impaired, but focused attention on the road is diminished and reaction time is slowed. Not exactly a formula for road safety.

Here is another sobering piece of information (pun intended). After seventeen hours without sleep, a driver has the same diminished reaction time as someone with a blood alcohol level of 0.05 mg. After twenty-one hours awake, you're at the illegal blood alcohol level of 0.08 mg. After twenty-four hours without sleep, you're at the equivalent of *twice* the illegal alcohol limit. Of course, if you also have alcohol in your system, it intensifies the problem.

Sleep deprivation doesn't just impair reaction time and judgement on the road. Add to this the number of home accidents, accidents on the job, mistakes made at work, poor business decisions, medical mishaps, and drug errors, and you start to get a sense of the enormity of the problem. Lack of sleep wreaks a stunning amount of damage on us, individually and collectively.

Tired people do not function well. Tired people are not resilient. They're less attentive and efficient; they make mistakes and have accidents; they're less creative problem solvers and more negative in their thinking. Doctors don't think as laterally when sleep deprived, which can

Tired people are not resilient.

affect their ability to make difficult diagnoses. In addition, tired people are not as creative in general. Since creativity and innovative thinking are the two most highly valued skill sets in today's workplace, these folks are starting every sleep-deprived day at a huge disadvantage. A tired office is an unproductive and unimaginative workplace.

In short, sleep deprivation affects how you feel and how you function.

Now, let's look at the inverse, when people do get the sleep they need. I continually hear testimonials about the benefits from my patients, but folks also sometimes send me emails with feedback after my presentations. Here are excerpts from two that stand out:

"It is not an overstatement to say that going to bed one half hour earlier every night has vastly improved the quality of my life! I am much calmer and better able to deal with the stresses of my job. That half hour of sleep has repaid itself exponentially. My life is much more balanced and I have even found the time to take up running again. Who would have thought that it might be that simple?"

"As an intelligent young man in my early twenties, I thought I was doing quite well. Your session made me realize that I do too much in my life — trying to balance school, work, and competitive sports as well as have a social life. For the past three nights, I have avoided watching late-night comedy and have gone to bed an hour earlier. This extra hour of sleep has allowed me to feel much more refreshed in the morning. The tenseness I was starting to have in my shoulders has nearly disappeared and I feel much more relaxed. This does not even begin to mention the improvement I have had in my concentration while at work and my natural ability to problem solve has come back. (I didn't realize it had gone away until I looked back at the last couple of months.)"

What about you? Are you getting the sleep you need on a regular basis? Do the above symptoms resonate with you? If so, it's time for some remedial action. More awareness leads to better choices.

CHAPTER 17

SLEEP DEBT

Sleep debt is the difference between the amount of sleep you *need* and the amount of sleep you *get*. If you need eight hours a night to function at your best and you get seven, you have a sleep debt of one hour. However, if that goes on for a week, you now have an accumulated sleep debt of seven hours. This is almost like losing an entire night's sleep each week. As we saw in the previous chapter, sleep debt affects your mental abilities considerably. It dulls thinking processes and slows reaction time. Losing four hours of sleep in one night can slow reaction time by as much as 45 percent.

Professional sports teams are "waking up" to this reality and addressing it. The Seattle Seahawks gave their players electronic wristbands that monitor the amount and quality of their sleep. Some hockey teams have adjusted their travel schedules, flying to the next city the morning following a game instead of taking an overnight flight. When elite athletes, even big tough football players, start paying attention to sleep, you know they realize its importance.

I play tennis. If I get behind in my sleep (which isn't often anymore), I make a lot more unforced errors than I do when I'm fully rested. And my reflexes for volleying at the net are noticeably quicker when I get the sleep I need. Even for an amateur, I feel I'm at the top of my game when my sleep requirements are met.

The good news about sleep debt is that we can repay it. *Sort of.* Our brains actually require that we do so. We can't go back and recover the lost sleep from four months ago, but we *can* repay recent sleep debt fairly readily. A few nights of full, uninterrupted sleep will usually do the trick. There are three ways to catch up.

The best and most physiological method is to go to bed earlier. Go to bed thirty minutes earlier for a night or two. Then add another half hour each night until you can wake up before (or without) your alarm, you feel well rested, and you have good daytime energy. For most adults, that will be about eight hours of sleep. The second way to repay the debt is to sleep in — preferably on the weekend so you don't lose your job by being late for work! A note of caution here: don't sleep longer than sixty to ninety extra minutes or it will throw off your body rhythm and you'll have trouble getting to sleep the next night.

The third way of paying back sleep debt is by taking a short nap. Doctors could never have gotten through medical training without grabbing quick catnaps, especially during or after being on call at night. Dr. James Maas coined the phrase "power nap" for these minisiestas. I was taking power naps for thirty years before I knew they had a name — and most of them were inadvertent! I'd drift off in class, at meetings, during concerts, while reading, and sometimes even with other people. When I'd come to, I'd look around and sheepishly say, "Oh, sorry. Was I gone long?" But after I got over my embarrassment, I'd notice that I was now awake, alert, and able to carry on. Eventually, I gave myself permission to take power naps when needed. They've been a lifesaver ever since — amazingly restorative.

Here are a few helpful tips. Limit the nap to twenty minutes. If you sleep longer, you will get into the deep sleep phase and often wake up feeling groggy. If you sleep more than twenty minutes, you're better off sleeping a full ninety minutes and going through an entire sleep cycle. The optimal time to nap is early to midafternoon because your body has a natural energy dip between 1 and 4 p.m. That's why the after-lunch siesta is such a physiological and healthy thing to do. If you nap in the evening, you might have trouble falling asleep later when you go to bed. I suggest sleeping in an upright or semireclining position. If you lie down and get too comfortable, you might have trouble waking up. I close my office door, put the phone on "Do Not Disturb," lean back in my tilt chair, put one foot up on the corner of my desk, and I'm gone. I set a little kitchen timer for twenty minutes so I don't oversleep. When I wake up refreshed, I get back to my work.

Napping is a hard sell in the workplace. Most people equate it with goofing off. Given all the benefits, though, it's unfortunate that napping has gotten such a bad rap. After all, if a short nap can reduce stress, replenish energy, restore attentiveness, and improve mood, why do we have such hang-ups about it? It's time to get smarter about the benefits and drop the cynical bias. If a twenty-minute coffee break is an accepted norm, if going out for a twenty-minute walk hardly raises an eyebrow, if even ducking out for a quick cigarette is viewed with understanding, then why does anyone care about twenty minutes of quick shut-eye? In all cases, people come back refreshed and ready to work again. Who cares how they refreshed themselves? In *The Art of Napping at Work,* authors Camille and Bill Anthony make an important distinction: napping *at* the job is not the same as napping *on* the job. Some enlightened workplaces such as Huffington Post even provide napping rooms because they realize the benefits to their employees.

> Napping *at* the job is not the same as napping *on* the job.

Nature's Way of Repaying Sleep Debt

If you don't repay sleep debt intentionally, your body will do it for you. And often at inconvenient times. Sometimes the brain goes to sleep for only a few seconds. You may not even realize it. You might continue what you're doing, but your brain has checked out in a quick attempt to repay some of the sleep debt you've amassed. These minislumbers are called "microsleeps," which Dr. William Dement defines as "uncontrollable and unpredictable bouts of sleep that happen faster than a seizure." Microsleeps can last as long as a minute or two but are often much shorter, even just a few seconds.

Depending on what you're doing at the time, the consequences can be devastating. If you just miss a few words of a lecture, or your handwriting gets sloppy for a line or two, it's no big deal. But what if you're driving a car? Say you have a ten-second microsleep while you're doing thirty miles per hour (forty-eight kilometres per hour). Your vehicle will cover a distance of 440 feet while you are effectively unconscious. That's one-and-a-half times longer than a football field, far enough for you to leave the road and hit a tree, or go over an embankment. In mere seconds, terrible things can happen, all because your brain is desperately trying to pay back the sleep debt you've accumulated. A lot of people think they know when they're about to fall asleep at the wheel. But, as Dr. Dement points out, drowsiness is not the first sign of impending sleep. It's the last thing that happens before you actually fall asleep.

Factors Affecting Sleep

In *The Promise of Sleep,* Dr. William Dement identifies three interrelated factors affecting sleep. I think of them as three points of a triangle. The first is our internal body clock. This is a built-in mechanism that tells us when to sleep and when to wake up. For most adults, cortisol levels fall at about 10 p.m. and melatonin, our natural sleep hormone, is secreted by the pineal gland in the brain. The reverse happens between 6 and 8 a.m., when melatonin levels fall and we get a surge of cortisol. This "clock-dependent alerting" is physiological, hard-wired, and has been part of human biology for thousands of years.

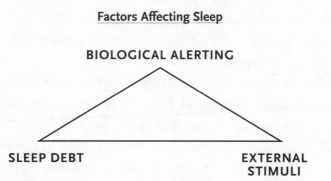

Factors Affecting Sleep

BIOLOGICAL ALERTING

SLEEP DEBT   **EXTERNAL STIMULI**

Dr. Colin Shapiro, a renowned sleep specialist at the University of Toronto, points out that melatonin actually rises at sunset (which varies throughout the year). So if melatonin pills are taken on prescription, it is not good practice to take them before bed because they have a hypnotic effect but not a chronobiotic effect (that is, they don't mirror the *body's* physiological timing of secretion, which is largely mediated by light and darkness).

The second factor is sleep debt. The greater the buildup, the stronger the urge to sleep. This explains why it takes about fifteen minutes to fall asleep when your body is fully rested (no accumulated sleep debt), but if you're sleep deprived (high sleep debt), you fall asleep in seconds or minutes.

The third factor is external stimulation. Noise, light, TV, lively music, an uncomfortable mattress, a restless (or amorous) bed partner, a ringing telephone, or incoming text messages (don't you just love that sound when you're drifting off?) — all of these things can interfere with sleep.

Any combination of these three things will affect your sleepiness or wakefulness. Ideally, you're in a quiet, dark, cool room, on a comfortable mattress at about 10 or 10:30 p.m., with a normal buildup of sleep debt. Your body will do the rest and you'll fall asleep. But, if you try to sleep at 8 p.m. in a college dorm with a lot of commotion going on, and especially if you've paid off some sleep debt with a late-afternoon nap, good luck! Sleep isn't going to happen.

You can apply the same triangle to daytime sleepiness. When I was in medical school, we had a lot of lectures that featured slides projected on a screen. This was before PowerPoint and LCD projectors so the room had to be dark. Each lecturer began with the same words: "Lights off, please. First slide." Five minutes later it seemed like half the class was asleep — especially if it was the first lecture after lunch! What was happening here? Our body clocks were set to "being awake" mode. There was noise in the room (someone talking through a microphone) and yet folks were asleep. The dark room was conducive to sleeping, but you still see this in fully lit rooms. The problem was that we'd built up a sufficient sleep debt that it overpowered the other two factors. This is why people can have trouble staying awake driving home at 5 p.m. in the summer — even with the windows open and the radio blaring — if they're carrying enough sleep debt.

Similarly, even with less sleep debt, you can get sleepy during the day if there isn't much external stimulation. Driving for hours on a fairly straight highway that doesn't have much interesting scenery can do the trick. Same thing if you're in a boring meeting or riding on an airplane droning along for hours, even during the day. All three factors affect your ability to sleep — or to stay awake.

> "There is no cure for sleepiness other than sleep."
> —Dr. William Dement

There is, however, a fourth factor that patients tell me about all the time: internal stimulation. We might picture the triangle now expanded to a rectangle.

One More Factor Affecting Sleep

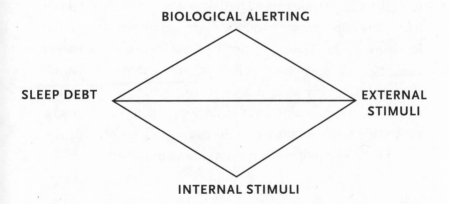

BIOLOGICAL ALERTING

SLEEP DEBT   EXTERNAL STIMULI

INTERNAL STIMULI

It's 11:30 p.m. so your body is biologically programmed for sleep. You're tired from a long day so you've built up a healthy sleep debt. The room is dark, cool, and quiet. The conditions are optimal for drifting off. Yet there you are, infuriatingly awake. What gives? Maybe you're worrying about your next mortgage payment or upset about an incident that happened during the evening. Or you're anxious about the presentation you'll be giving tomorrow afternoon. Or you're thinking of all the things you have to do tomorrow and hoping you won't forget to buy milk. Many busy folks have lots of lists in their mental storage cabinet: kids' activities, meal menus, work assignments, weekend plans for the family. There's a lot to keep track of—but the timing is lousy. The little voice in your head is robbing you of sleep. Other internal stimuli include your painful shoulder or arthritic hip, hot flashes or night sweats, the sunburn or itchy rash you just acquired that you didn't notice during the day but now they're front and centre.

Lastly, there is simply the worry about not being *able* to fall asleep or the exasperation when you *can't*. The internal conversation goes something like this: *I can't fall asleep. What if I'm awake half the night? I'll be a walking zombie tomorrow. I have to get to sleep. This is ridiculous!* The longer it takes to fall asleep, the more frustrated you get. And the more aggravated you get, the less likely you are to drift off. Some people try to *will* themselves to sleep. They concentrate on it. They *work* at it. All to no avail. Want to know why? Sleep is an involuntary function. You can't will yourself to sleep. All you can do is get out of your own way, set a stage that's conducive to sleep, and let your body do the rest. That's why proper sleep habits are so important.

Sleep Disorders

What if you do everything right, get your eight hours a night, and still don't feel rested and refreshed? There's a high likelihood that you have a sleep disorder. You're getting the *quantity* of sleep you need, but not the *quality* you require. Sleep researchers have identified more than seventy sleep disorders, but the two most common ones are obstructive sleep apnea (OSA) and restless legs syndrome (RLS).

Obstructive Sleep Apnea (OSA)

In *The Promise of Sleep*, Dr. William Dement says that every night more than fifty million Americans stop breathing. How's that for attention-grabbing? The condition is called apnea (literally "absence of breath") and it affects up to 10 percent of the population. First identified in 1965, obstructive sleep apnea is widespread, significant, and almost totally overlooked or ignored. According to Dr. Dement, "In all of medicine, I can't think of a single other serious condition that is so common, life-threatening, treatable, and yet so unrecognized." It predisposes us to high blood pressure, heart disease, strokes, and, in men, impotence. It leads to daytime sleepiness, sluggishness, cognitive and memory impairment, headaches, and the risk of microsleeps that can cause accidents, especially when driving. *Depression* can even result from the chronic sleep deprivation of OSA.

What obstructs the breathing? When we're asleep, our throat muscles relax and tend to collapse inward when we take a breath. There's also a tendency for the tongue to fall back and block the airway. As carbon dioxide builds up and blood oxygen levels fall, we try to breathe in, but the airway is obstructed. Our brains literally have to wake us up to get us breathing again. But we do this without conscious awareness. People with OSA repeatedly fight for breath all night long without ever knowing it. Only a clinical observer or bed partner can see what's going on. The diagnosis is confirmed with a sleep study.

Are you at risk? If you snore, are overweight, have high blood pressure, and have nonrestorative sleep (that is, you don't feel rested after a full night of sleep), there's a good chance you have OSA. Alcohol and sedatives are risk factors because they further relax the throat muscles. Enlarged tonsils and adenoids or a naturally small airway can also predispose a person to apnea. It's about three times more common in men, but the prevalence is roughly equal in women after menopause. OSA affects millions of people.

What's the treatment? Weight loss and strict avoidance of alcohol and sedatives in the evening are essential first steps in any treatment regimen. The gold standard of treatment is a continuous positive airway pressure (CPAP) machine that blows air through the nose or mouth and keeps the airway open. A simpler solution is a dental appliance that moves the jaw forward and helps splint or tighten the muscle wall of the throat, but it's not effective for everyone. For millions of people who had been profoundly tired and often depressed, treatment of OSA has given them back their lives.

Restless Legs Syndrome (RLS)

The hallmark of this syndrome is uncomfortable and sometimes painful feelings in the legs. This creates a desire to move the legs, which then causes difficulty sleeping. When symptoms occur, victims vigorously flex, stretch, and cross their legs to ease their discomfort. The prevalence increases with age but may occur in children. There appears to be no gender difference. The basic cause is unknown.

According to Dr. Dement, it's very easy to spot: "We simply ask, 'Do you have creepy, crawly feelings in your legs when you are sitting or lying that go away when you walk about and that are worse at night?'" It affects fifteen to twenty million Americans. The RLS Foundation conservatively estimates the prevalence at 5 percent of the population. Other estimates are closer to 10 percent. Medication is available as a treatment option, but sufferers are also encouraged to drink more water (and less alcohol) in the evening, and refrain from keeping the legs elevated before bedtime (say, for instance, when reading or watching television). Massaging the leg muscles and stretching at bedtime can also help.

Why Are People So Reluctant to Get the Sleep They Need?

I've heard the litany of reasons and excuses for people not getting enough sleep:

- "I have too much to do"
- "I don't want to miss anything" (FOMO — fear of missing out)
- "Late night is the only quiet time I have to myself"
- "I'm a night owl"
- "I can't unwind until midnight"
- "My spouse likes to stay up late and wants me to join them"
- "Sleep is a waste of time"
- "Sleep is for wimps"

- "I'm afraid that if I go to sleep, I might not wake up on time in the morning"

But there's another pervasive factor at play: the twenty-four-hour culture. People are working longer than they were twenty years ago and they're staying up later to finish home chores or work tasks, answer emails, or surf the Internet. After-hours clubs abound. Stores are open at all hours — all-night groceries, doughnut shops, pharmacies, even twenty-four-hour banking. There are also twenty-four-hour fitness centres, which seems a strange biological conflict—people are exercising at exactly the time that they're biologically programmed to be sleeping. Then there are shift workers (about 20 percent of the American labour force) who toil in factories, hospitals, police departments, ambulance services, media outlets and other round-the-clock enterprises. The price being paid by these workers is considerable.

> We have to stop wearing sleep deprivation as a sign of strength and a badge of honour.

CHAPTER 18

WHAT'S THE SOLUTION?

What's the prescription to fix this situation? There's a simple answer and one that's more complex. The simple answer is to *get the sleep you need on a regular basis*. It's as plain as the nose on your face. And yet people resist the obvious.

It reminds me of the story about a man who's complaining about sore feet. His friend asks, "What's the problem?" to which the guy replies, "I've got size 9 feet and I'm wearing size 8 shoes." His friend counters, "Duh! If you know what the problem is, why don't you just go out and buy shoes that fit?" Mr. Sore Feet responds, "Yeah, that's the logical answer. But it's not that simple. I hate my job. My car is falling apart. My girlfriend's not talking to me. To be honest, the only pleasure I get anymore is when I go home at night and take off my shoes!"

That is the worst joke I know — but it makes an important point. Sometimes the answer to a problem is obvious. The solution to our chronic, societal sleep deprivation is evident and clear. It's staring us right in the face. Each of us can *choose* to get the sleep we need.

The more complex issue is *how* to get that sleep on a regular basis. Good sleep habits are called "sleep hygiene." Here are some guidelines:

Rules to Sleep By

1. Aim for at least eight hours per night (unless you truly
    know you need less).

2. As much as possible, go to bed and wake up at the same
    time every day. Our bodies love rhythm and routine. As
    sleep expert Dr. James Maas says, "You only have one
    body clock. You don't have one for weekdays and one for
    weekends."

3. Develop a bedtime routine to wind down (take a bath,
    read, listen to soft music, etc.). The reason for taking a
    hot bath at bedtime is a bit of a paradox. It's not to make
    you warm and toasty. It works in actually *lowering* body
    temperature. After the bath, your body cools down, which
    prepares you for sleep. Dropping your temperature from
    warm to cold is the key.

4. Clear your mind of problems and worries. Think calm and
    pleasant thoughts.

5. Prepare an agenda or to-do list for the next day before
    going to bed so you can clear your mind for sleep. If you're
    worrying about something, write it down and decide to
    deal with it the following day.

6. Don't watch TV in your bedroom and especially not right
    before bedtime. Better yet, remove the TV altogether.
    The bedroom should be for sleep and sex only; it's not an
    entertainment centre.

IF A TROUBLED MIND is preventing you from falling asleep, try the following exercise, called "creative worrying." Take a piece of paper and write down answers to the following questions:

- What is your greatest fear at this moment?

- What is the likelihood of it coming to pass?

- If it did, what would you do to handle it?

- What can you do right now to either prevent it from happening or to prepare for it?

Once you've written down your answers, you now have a game plan for dealing with the problem. Further worry will serve no further purpose, so you might as well put it away and go to sleep.

7. Avoid all screens (laptops, tablets, smartphones, e-readers) in the hour before bedtime. The light shining into your eyes signals the brain to stay awake and suppresses the release of melatonin. If you absolutely have to read on a screen in bed, note that there are now apps and glasses that block the blue light that stimulates wakefulness.

8. Don't do work-related activities in the bedroom, especially in the evening.

9. Avoid caffeine within eight to ten hours of bedtime — it fragments your sleep cycles, blocking deep restorative sleep.

10. Avoid exertion and strenuous exercise within three hours of bedtime. Mild to moderate activity is fine, but vigorous

exercise stimulates adrenalin release that can energize
your body for hours.

11. Avoid heavy meals within three hours of bedtime.

12. Avoid alcohol within three hours of bedtime. It fragments
    both deep sleep and REM (dream) sleep and leads to
    early-morning wakening (the "rebound effect"). It also
    suppresses the release of growth hormone.

13. Avoid sleeping pills. They can lead to psychological
    dependence or even physical addiction.

14. Don't nap if you have trouble sleeping at night.

15. Don't nap in the evening.

16. Do some form of exercise or physical activity during the
    day. This enhances both the duration and the quality of
    your sleep.

17. Create a conducive sleep environment (a dark, quiet, and
    cool room).

18. Get a comfortable but firm mattress and a good,
    supportive pillow.

19. A small snack an hour before bedtime may be helpful,
    especially if it includes milk, which is a natural source of
    tryptophan, a sleep-enhancing amino acid.

20. If you have trouble getting to sleep for more than half an hour, get up and do something calming until you feel sleepy. Then return to bed.

Insomnia: What If You *Can't* Sleep?

There are two reasons why people aren't getting enough sleep. The first is not enough hours lying horizontal between the covers on a comfortable mattress in a cool, dark room. In other words, not making adequate time for sleep. The second reason is not being *able* to sleep. Despite their best intentions, about 20 percent of the population suffers from insomnia.

There are three kinds of insomnia: trouble falling asleep ("sleep induction"), trouble staying asleep ("sleep maintenance" — frequent awakenings), and early-morning waking (for example, around 5 or 5:30 a.m.). Many people have more than one of these sleep disorders, which then have a multiplier effect.

All the causes of insomnia are too numerous to mention, but here are some common ones that I see in my practice:

- **Stress and worry.**
  People can't fall asleep because they're in a state of turmoil regarding work issues, fretting about finances, worrying about a relationship, or upset about an argument close to bedtime. Or they wake up in the night and start stewing about a problem or thinking about all the things they have to do the next day.

- **Too much stimulation at bedtime.**
  You watch the final period of an exciting basketball game and then try to fall asleep—which isn't going to happen with all that adrenalin running around your body. I used to play hockey on Wednesday nights. Our ice time was 10 p.m. I'd drag myself off the ice at 11:30 p.m. feeling exhausted. But I was also exhilarated. I'd be wired till one o'clock in the morning. It was that adrenalin and those feel-good beta endorphins, which made sleep impossible.

- **Too much noise, light, heat, or cold.**
  If the climate in your bedroom is not conducive to sleep, you'll have trouble drifting off. Other external stimuli include a restless or snoring bed partner, a telephone ringing, or a baby crying just as you're nodding off.

- **Insufficient sleep debt.**
  Here's a story I hear all too often. A patient tells me he lies down to watch TV in the evening and falls asleep on the sofa. After an hour or two, he wakes up, drags himself to bed—and then lies there, infuriatingly awake, unable to get back to sleep. What happened? He paid off some of his sleep debt with his ill-timed power nap, thus removing one of the main drivers for quality sleep. This often becomes a cycle. The next evening the guy is tired from insufficient sleep the previous night, so he crashes on the couch to watch TV, conks out for a while, and thus sabotages his *next* night's sleep. Seeing this pattern (more awareness) can lead to better choices (no evening siesta).

- **Caffeine or a large meal close to bedtime.**
  Caffeine stimulates the release of adrenalin and cortisol, both of which oppose sleep. It also blocks a natural relaxant in the brain called adenosine. It's the perfect storm to prevent sleep from occurring. Similarly, foods rich in fat stimulate cortisol secretion. Foods high in protein stimulate our wake-up hormones. So, if you're going to eat late, eat light. Soup and salad or pasta (carbohydrates are sleep inducers) would be much better choices. Or just have a bowl of cereal and a banana (milk and bananas contain tryptophan, another sleep enhancer).

  > If you're going to eat late, eat light.

- **Alcohol and fluids in the evening.**
  A group of my high school pals have dinner together a few times a year, a cherished ritual. At one dinner during the year I turned fifty, we'd barely sat down when one of them asked, "How often do you guys have to get up at night to pee?" I remember thinking, *Oh, please! Is it starting already? Conversations about ailments and getting older?* (This is sometimes known as the "organ recital.") Fortunately, we've mostly avoided that track at our subsequent dinners.

  The fact is that male prostate glands enlarge with age, impairing bladder emptying and leading to having to get up during the night to pass water. That's biology. But two things make it worse: drinking fluids in the evening and drinking alcohol, which is a diuretic and therefore adds to the problem. (Caffeine is also a diuretic and has the same effect.) The solution is to cut down on fluids in the evening and avoid alcohol within three hours of bedtime. I have a raft of grateful patients who have followed this simple advice with wonderful results. The first time they sleep right through the night is like a gift from the gods.

- **Hot flashes and sweats.**
  Women in their middle years can be infuriated by the onset of menopausal symptoms that make getting to sleep or staying asleep frustratingly difficult. There are herbal and naturopathic remedies available for this, as well as hormone replacement therapies for those who choose to pursue this with their doctor.

- **Depression.**
  Generally speaking, anxiety makes it difficult to *fall* asleep, but depression makes it hard to *stay* asleep. People suffering from depression report frequent wakening through the night and/or early-morning wakening. If this pattern emerges for you, check it out with your doctor.

- **Brain waves.**
  I'm lucky. I rarely have trouble sleeping and I rarely have disturbing dreams. But one thing that can interfere with my sleep is when I get good ideas in the middle of the night. This happens especially if I'm working on a book or a new presentation. My mind seems to generate great ideas during the night. There's a reason for that. There are three times when our conscious and subconscious minds come closest together: just as we fall asleep, just as we wake up, and during meditation. This can lead to great insights, creative and innovative thinking, and solutions to perplexing problems. But it also wakes you up, especially if you want to capture the idea before

it disappears. A helpful solution is to quickly write down your thoughts—in the dark—on a pad of paper by your bedside.

Prescriptions for Insomnia

If you have trouble *falling* sleep, refer to the sleep hygiene guidelines on page 136. The other issue that perplexes many people is how to get *back* to sleep if they wake up at night. Here are some suggestions:

- **Stay in bed.**
  Unless you have to go to the bathroom, answer the phone, tend to a crying child, or do something similar, don't get up. The less interference to your resting state, the better.

- **Don't turn on a light.**
  Light is the main signal to the brain that it's time to wake up. Keep the lights off and your eyes closed, reinforcing the signal to the brain that it's still sleep time and promoting the transition back to sleep.

Here's a tip for the guys: lower the toilet seat and sit down. That way you can stay half-asleep while you empty your bladder—eliminating the worry about where you're aiming—then slip back to bed while you're still in that twilight haze that helps you drift back to sleep.

- **If you have to get up to use the bathroom, don't turn on the light.**
  Learn to walk to the bathroom with your eyelids at half-mast, do your business, and get back into bed without fully waking up.

- **Don't look at the clock.**
  When patients tell me they woke up at 3:13 or 4:23 a.m., I know they don't have

incredible time-estimating capacities. They looked at their fluorescent, digital, glow-in-the-dark clocks. Don't do that. Turn the sucker toward the wall. Don't try to find out what time it is. That extra bit of stimulation just moves you closer to full consciousness. If it's still dark and your alarm hasn't gone off yet, it doesn't matter what time it is. (By the way, the light from some of these luminous digital clocks is enough to get through your closed eyelids and trick the brain into thinking it's light outside.) The same advice applies to cell phones.

- **Don't start thinking.**
  A lot of people tell me that as soon as they wake up in the middle of the night, they start thinking—about work, about things they have to do the next day, about money, about their kids, etc. If you allow yourself to engage in those internal conversations, you raise your level of consciousness and pull yourself further away from sleep. Resist the temptation to let your mind get in gear.

- **Write down your brilliant ideas.**
  As noted in the list of causes of sleep disruption, you might get a sudden brain wave as you wake in the night. While the timing is slightly inconvenient, these insights or creative thoughts can be very valuable. Don't ignore them or trust that you'll remember them in the morning. Instead, write them down. This is one exception to the don't-start-thinking rule. The thought is already there. Don't engage with it. Just capture it—then let it go and drift back to sleep. Keep a pen and paper by the bedside. Don't turn on the light. Just write it down and flesh it out in the morning. I've gotten some of

my best ideas this way—and it's fun trying to decipher my
midnight scrawl the next day.

- **Remember—and go back to—your dream.**
This is a trick I discovered years ago and was surprised to
find how many others use it as well. Here's the deal: If you
wake up, pay attention to what you were dreaming about.
Then hold it in your mind while you go to the bathroom.
It requires discipline and you have to do it quickly because
dream content fades within seconds. Then, when you return
to bed, go back into your dream (sort of like "Gee, I'd like to
finish the movie"). You will fall asleep quickly. I don't know
why this works, but it absolutely does. It seems to contradict
my don't-start-thinking rule, but for some reason it's not
the same as getting your brain fully into gear. It's more like
sliding back into the haze. Maybe it has something to do
with suggestibility. One note of caution: Do not try this if
you were having a nightmare! Don't say to yourself, *Wow,
was that scary! I wonder what happens next!*

- **Use relaxation techniques.**
One of the simplest ways to quiet your mind when it gets
too busy is to focus on your breathing—in and out, in and
out. It lulls you into a semihypnotic state that encourages
sleep. I quietly count the breaths as I do this. "In and out.
One. In and out. Two." I've never reached ten before falling
back to sleep. Another strategy is to slowly count backward
from 100 or to count sheep. Yet another technique is to
focus on muscle groups and relax them in sequence. Start
with the muscles in your toes. Then relax the muscles in
your feet, followed by your ankles, calf muscles, knees,

thighs, etc. Slowly work your way up your body to your neck, head, and even your eyelids. One more way to settle yourself and invite sleep is to imagine being in a calm, pleasant scene. My favourite is the beach on Paradise Island in the Bahamas. I can put myself there mentally within seconds, imagining the fine white sand, the turquoise water, the green palm trees, the blue sky, the bright sun. Throw in a gentle breeze and I'm back in slumberland.

- **If you simply can't go back to sleep, get up.**
  There are times when nothing seems to work. You're feeling restless and frustrated, you're tossing and turning, and your mind won't shut off. If that happens, get out of bed and go into another room. Read, listen to soft music, have a bowl of cereal, or maybe even make some notes about what's on your mind. Keep the light low and don't turn on the TV or your computer. Then, when you start to finally feel tired again, go back to bed—and to sleep.

Summary

Every organism, regardless of size, goes through cycles of activity and rest—even the single-cell amoeba. Every animal has to sleep. Lions sleep fourteen to eighteen hours a day, sometimes up to twenty if it's very hot. Talk about a short workday! I guess if you're king of the jungle, you can do pretty much whatever you want. Even the busy beaver sleeps eleven hours a day. Elephants only need four hours, even though they're enormous. Horses only get three. It's the luck of the biological draw. Humans drew the card that said eight. It's simply the way it is. That's the way we're designed and wired. And it's not going to change any time soon.

So we have two choices: we either get the sleep we need or we don't. If we do, we will function optimally, feel great, and enjoy better health. If we don't, we will suffer physically (fatigue, infections, weight gain), mentally (impaired memory, concentration, and judgement), and emotionally (low mood, depression), and perform less well at our jobs. That's the choice we all make every day.

It seems that most of us are trying to shortchange nature to see if we can get away with less. We're sleeping about two hours less than our ancestors did one hundred years ago. Whether we stay up late to read, watch TV, study, party, play sports, go to the movies, or do shift work, we are living in conflict with our own biology. The cost to us as individuals and as a society is considerable. It's time to wake up — and go to sleep!

SECTION 4

THE VALUES YOU ESPOUSE
VS.
THE VALUES YOU LIVE

CHAPTER 19

WHAT YOU SAY VS. WHAT YOU DO

Baron Gottfried von Cramm is probably the best tennis player you've never heard of. In the 1930s, he was the second-best tennis player in the world and possibly the greatest German player ever. However, he was known not only for his outstanding physical skill but also for his remarkable sportsmanship. Nowhere was this better illustrated than on the No. 1 Court at Wimbledon in 1935.

In his book *A Terrible Splendor*, Marshall Jon Fisher wrote about the life and career of von Cramm and described the iconic moment in the 1935 Davis Cup challenge round that cemented his reputation as "the Gentleman of Wimbledon." In the pivotal doubles match against the Americans, Cramm had played magnificently, bringing him and his teammate to match point five times. With the match again on the line, his partner, Kai Lund, appeared to hit a winning shot to give Germany a sixth match point. But Cramm, "the soul of chivalry" as one observer described him, walked over to the umpire and calmly informed him that the ball had grazed his own racket before Lund had hit it. Neither the umpire nor any of the other players had noticed. The Americans went on to win the point and the match, advancing past the Germans to the next round.

When later criticized for his famous tipped-ball admission, Cramm replied, "Tennis is a gentleman's game and that's the way I've played it ever since I picked up my first racket. Do you think that I would sleep tonight knowing that the ball had touched my racket without my saying so? Never, because I would be violating every principle I think this game stands for. On the contrary, I don't think I'm letting the German people down. I think I'm doing them credit."

In that single moment, Gottfried von Cramm demonstrated that he valued honour over victory. He valued integrity and fair play over winning when he alone knew that the victory would have been tainted. This is a classic example of a man who is clear about his values. Equally important, he had the courage to *live* his values, even when it was inconvenient and costly. That instantaneous decision was totally congruent with who he was as an athlete and as a person.

The world of sports abounds with similar stories. In 1925, Bobby Jones, the reigning golf champion in the 1920s, called a penalty on himself that cost him a tournament championship. In the 1936 Olympics in Berlin, German long jumper Luz Long helped his opponent, Jesse Owens, avoid a third foot fault that would have disqualified the American. Owens won the gold medal on his final jump; Long came in second—a remarkable example of the Olympic ideal at its best. More recently, Canadian speed skater Gilmore Junio qualified for the thousand-metre finals at the 2014 Winter Olympics but voluntarily stepped aside to allow his veteran teammate, Denny Morrison, to compete in his place. Morrison won the silver medal; Junio won the hearts of all Canadians and the respect of the international sporting world.

Contrast those examples of integrity with the behaviour of disgraced athletes like cyclist Lance Armstrong and baseball player Alex Rodriguez, who chose winning, money, and fame over honesty by using performance-enhancing drugs to cheat their way to victory—and then lied about it for years after.

Values Conflict and Stress

Values conflicts are at the heart of many stressful situations. Folks often have to make decisions that may get them ahead but don't sit well with their conscience. That internal discord is often a source of stress that I hear about from my patients. One woman struggled with an edict from her boss to keep selling their software even though there were glitches that hadn't yet been resolved. A man was pushed to sell his company's product to new customers and to ignore complaints from current clients who were getting lousy service when there were problems. *He* valued after-sales service while his company was only about volume, sales, and revenue. What he was directed to do had a steadily corrosive effect on his enthusiasm for work but, even worse, on his spirit and morale. It was in direct conflict with his own principles and eventually would have been soul destroying if he had stayed there. He finally quit when the moral dissonance became unacceptable.

I wonder how many bank employees prior to the economic collapse in 2008 suffered the same internal struggle when they were approving mortgages for home buyers whom they *knew* would never be able to keep up the payments. Similarly, people who were peddling subprime mortgages and junk bonds in the years leading up to the meltdown may have been making a ton of money on commissions and bonuses, but I'll bet some of them weren't sleeping so well at night.

On a related note, a recent CBC story reported tellers at a major Canadian bank were being pressured to push customers to sign up for services they didn't need — products such as overdraft protection, credit cards, and lines of credit. Their title was changed from "customer service reps" to "front-line advisors" and they were given quarterly sales goals to meet or risk losing their jobs. One teller said, "I'm in survival mode now. It's a choice between keeping my job and feeding my family—or doing what's right for the customer." Another said, "I have to put my ethics aside and not do what's right for the customer. You don't know what it's like to go to bed at night, knowing your job is now to set people up for financial failure." Another said the relentless pressure to meet sales numbers was so strong they had to go on medical leave. Several other tellers said they quit their jobs because the pressure to push products was so extreme.

Early in my medical career I worked briefly at a large medical clinic in Toronto. One day a healthy young man came in for a smallpox vaccination. Those were the days before smallpox was eradicated; at that time, people needed certification of vaccination in order to travel abroad. The procedure was quite simple—spreading a small amount of vaccine on the upper arm and then using a needle to make a few scratches in the skin for the vaccine to be absorbed. I asked one of the older doctors what the fee was for doing this procedure. I was taken aback by his reply.

"The fee is three dollars, but you don't charge three dollars."

"What do you mean?" I asked.

"You find something wrong with the patient and then you bill six dollars for a minor assessment."

"But the guy's twenty-three years old and perfectly healthy. He has no physical complaints."

"So you look for something. If he's got flat feet, you write the diagnosis as *pes planus*. If he's losing his hair, you write alopecia."

"But what if there's nothing to find?"

"Just keep looking. Nobody's perfect."

That would have been a great line in a sitcom, but he was

serious. Hiding my sarcasm, I thanked him for his sage advice and proceeded to submit the claim for three dollars. I was young, naive, and idealistic. (I'm now older and wiser, but still idealistic.) I couldn't believe that anyone would misrepresent the work done when submitting a claim to the government insurance plan. Aside from the morality issue, it occurred to me that if I ever got audited I would have to do some pretty fast talking to explain myself. This fear was reinforced when I told a former classmate the story. He said to me, "You're working *where?* You've got to get out of there. They've already been audited once by the College of Physicians and Surgeons and I think they're being audited again." I had also told him two other stories about the dubious medical and billing practices of this group, but they were things that hadn't affected me directly. His reaction reinforced my discomfort and told me that it was time to move on. Shortly after, I handed in my resignation.

When we talk about values, what is it we're actually referring to? In their classic book, *Your Money or Your Life*, authors Joe Dominguez and Vicki Robin state that "our values are those principles and qualities that matter to us, that are really important to our sense of well-being. On one level, values are the ideas and beliefs on which we base our decisions. They are like an invisible DNA, made up of our sense of right and wrong, that structures our choices." I know a number of people who turned down transfers or promotions at work because they required moving to another city when their teenage children were in high school. This is an example of making family a priority over career. Others have taken less prestigious or lucrative jobs closer to home in order to reduce commuting time and spend more of that time with their families. A clear awareness of our own values helps us to make better choices in our lives.

I think of values in three different ways: principles, priorities, and preferences. In the following chapters, we'll look at each of them in turn.

CHAPTER 20

PRINCIPLES

Morality, Honesty, Integrity, Trust, Authenticity

Roger Mellott was a stress specialist in Louisiana. He was once asked to describe the essence of stress management in one sentence. He did it in seven words: "Identify your values and support them behaviourally." In other words, decide what is important to you and then design and live your life in a way that supports and reflects those values. We often think of integrity as a reflection of character and honesty. But it can also be viewed as an alignment of values with action, an *integration* of the two. If you live in a way that is consistent with your own values, life will usually be less conflicted and decisions easier to make. More awareness leads to better choices.

When your decisions, behaviour, and life choices are in conflict with your own underlying values, you will usually experience increased stress. When people are pushed into situations of moral conflict, they pay a high price in terms of cognitive dissonance. When asked to compromise their personal values, they often experience anguish and feel demoralized, even angry. Some people make the difficult choice to resist and risk unpleasant consequences. Others acquiesce and pay a painful cost internally. Either way it's an unpleasant, often terrible, bind to be in.

We're living in a world where ethics, morality, and integrity seem to be expendable in some people's attempts to get ahead — whether the pursuit is in academics, politics, the workplace, sports, journalism, entertainment, or just everyday interpersonal relationships. People are tempted to compromise their principles to get ahead, win an election, get a promotion, win a prize, etc. Cheating, plagiarism, dirty tricks, lying, breaking your word — sometimes it seems everything is up for grabs in our highly competitive, dog-eat-dog world.

The Ford Pinto was known by its manufacturer to have a dangerous design flaw that resulted in exploding gas tanks mounted in the rear. Between 1971 and 1978, the Pinto was responsible for a number of fire-related deaths. Ford put the figure at twenty-three; its critics say the figure was closer to 500. But it took litigation in response to those deaths to get Ford to admit the problem and fix it. Aside from the company's decision to continue production of the car, I've often wondered about the internal conflict that the executives who knew about the problem must have experienced. To say nothing of the engineers who were mandated to keep producing the cars despite the mounting evidence of risk to drivers and passengers. More recently, Volkswagen tarnished its image with an exhaust-emissions scandal. When even hugely profitable, iconic companies cut corners or cheat to make even *more* money, it gives all of us pause for thought about what's going on.

I think most people still have a pretty good moral compass when it comes to making decisions. It's called a conscience. Early in his career, a friend of mine accepted a job on a handshake. Soon after, he got a better offer from another company. But he declined because he had given his word. He paid a financial price for that decision, but it came from an inner sense of honour and integrity that served him well over the course of his life. It came from being true to who he was. He stayed in that job for over thirty years. Because of his character, he had a sterling reputation and was trusted and beloved by those who knew him and dealt with him in business. What's *that* worth on the open market? He also slept well at night.

We still hear good-news stories about people returning wallets or bundles of money that they've found. Folks return money sent to them in error by government agencies. Salespeople share commissions when they know that someone else helped to seal a deal. Restaurant customers point it out to servers when they aren't charged for the wine or dessert. Extramarital affairs often end when the guilt and stress experienced by one of the partners indicates the need to return to their moral centre. People decline to get involved in shady deals or enterprises, even when they're sure they'd get away with it. The "sniff test" is a good way to decide when to participate in some venture—and when *not* to. Some things just don't *feel* good. We all do better when we listen to our instincts and feelings. Our gut will usually tell us what's right and wrong, even if our head leads us astray and rationalizes a decision that really doesn't feel good.

What's the Solution?

1. **Do the right thing.**

   It's not always easy to stand up for your principles. You might encounter disagreement, social pressure, or even authoritative demands to conform. But standing firm can leave you feeling stronger, might earn you the respect of others, and might also make a difference in the very situation you're facing.

   Lynden Dorval was a physics teacher at Ross Sheppard High School in Edmonton, Alberta. He had an unblemished record for thirty-three years until he dared to do something unthinkable: he gave zeroes to students who didn't hand in assignments or who didn't take tests. His logic was clear: If you don't do the work, how can you expect to receive a grade? Unfortunately, his actions went against a no-zeroes school policy. To me, it's bad enough that schools rarely fail students anymore, even when they can't do the work — it's called "social promotion" — but to have to give a grade for work not done at all pushes the boundaries of bizarre thinking to new heights of absurdity.

> "Do the right thing. It will gratify some people and astonish the rest."
> — Mark Twain

In 2012, Dorval was suspended for his principled and courageous stand against a policy that made no sense to him. In an interview with the CBC, he said, "I'd never been asked to do anything this *dumb*. And I just said I can't *do* it. It was as simple as that." Four months later, he was fired. He later appealed his termination and won. In its decision, the Board of Reference wrote, "The basis for the suspension appeared to be that the principal viewed any form of dissent as insubordination which was not to be tolerated, despite repeated efforts by teachers to explain why the directive interfered with their professional judgement and could result in illegitimate outcomes." Dorval concluded, "Sometimes standing up for something has an effect. It actually works. It was just something that was the right thing to do." Not only did Dorval live his values, his case empowered another high school to publicly and proudly oppose the no-zeroes policy.

"Referability Habits": Good Rules to Live By If You're in Business

Living by a good set of values is its own reward in terms of self-respect. But it can have practical benefits as well. Dan Sullivan runs a coaching company for entrepreneurs called The Strategic Coach®. In the business world, there are two key measures of success: return business from old clients and new customers from word-of-mouth. Dan developed what he calls his four "referability habits." Your work or services may be stellar, but if you want people to refer you to their friends and family, there are four basic things you also need to do:

- Show up on time.

- Do what you say.

- Finish what you start.

- Say please and thank you.

Pretty simple guidelines for business success — and each represents a piece of integrity and personal values.

My Uncle Aaron's Lesson about Values

In 1983, one of my aunts passed away, and a few months later, my uncle asked me if I would like to have her car. Since my own vehicle was on its last legs (or wheels), I gratefully accepted his offer. We arranged for him to drive the car to Oakville, where I live, and then I would drive him back to his home in Toronto. I learned a wonderful lesson about values that day.

On the appointed Saturday morning, he called to tell me he needed a couple of hours to get the cruise control fixed and to fill the car with gas. I said to him, "Chalkie, you're already doing me an enormous favour. Let *me* fix the cruise control. Let *me* fill the car with gas." He then informed me of a wise Yiddish saying that I've never forgotten: "When you give, give with a whole hand." In other words, when you do something for someone, do it in as complete and gracious a way as possible. This was not only his philosophy but the way he lived his life.

I drove that car for only two years, but the lesson I learned that morning has stayed with me ever since. It was one of my uncle's values, and because he *lived* his values, he behaved in a way that was *congruent* with that philosophy.

2. **Live your authentic self.**

Murray was a very bright, talented, successful, warm, and funny guy with a big smile and a bigger heart. He was also bald. Except most people didn't know that—including me. It turns out Murray had one of the best toupees I ever saw— actually *never* saw because it was so good. That's how he presented himself to the world, until the day when it all unravelled in a moment of truth.

He was crossing a busy street in Montreal with some of his professional colleagues when a heavy wind came up. You can probably guess the rest. His rug flew off and suddenly he was someone else whom none of them had ever seen before. Talk about being busted! And embarrassed and humiliated. That's the day he decided to just be who he was. It turned out to be a whole lot easier than hiding his pate and feeling a tad anxious that someday he'd be found out. All his wonderful characteristics were still there and everyone loved him just as much as before, but I suspect that he was a lot more relaxed after that.

Being yourself is usually a lot easier than trying to be something or someone you're not. It's about being comfortable in your own skin. It's a better fit when you wear your own clothes than when you try to fit into someone else's. More awareness leads to better choices.

3. Remember that honesty goes a long way.

Larry Adler was a world-renowned virtuoso harmonica player in the mid-twentieth century. He was also a wonderful storyteller. I saw him perform at the National Arts Centre in Ottawa in the 1970s and he was fabulous. He told a story about how he got started in show business.

As a young teenager, he used to hang around stage doors of Broadway theatres. Whenever anyone walked in or out he would play a few bars on his harmonica and hope someone would notice him. One day a man heard him out in the alley at the Winter Garden Theatre where Paul "Pops" Whiteman and his orchestra were performing. Whiteman was one of the most famous bandleaders in America at the time. The man heard Larry playing and said, "Hey, kid, you're pretty good. Do you want to come in and meet Pops?"

> "If you tell the truth, you don't have to remember anything." — Mark Twain

The excited Larry Adler said, "Sure."

So the man took Larry into Whiteman's dressing room. It was after a performance and Whiteman was sitting in his bathrobe and schmoozing with friends sitting around the room. The man brought Larry into the room and said,

"Hey, Pops, I found this kid out in the alley playing the harmonica. He's pretty good so I thought I'd bring him in to meet you."

Whiteman asked, "What kind of music do you play, kid?"

Larry replied, "I can play anything."

So Whiteman asked him to play "Rhapsody in Blue," a famous piece of orchestral music at the time, composed by George Gershwin.

Larry didn't know how to play "Rhapsody in Blue." But he had just told Whiteman that he could play *anything*. He couldn't admit that he'd exaggerated, so he said to him, "Uh, I don't really *like* 'Rhapsody in Blue.'"

Upon hearing this, Whiteman smiled at one of the guys in the room and said, "Do you hear that, Gershwin? He doesn't like 'Rhapsody in Blue'!"

Adler told several stories about himself that night. But the Gershwin story stayed with me all these years as a humorous example of what can happen when we fudge the truth.

Honesty is a pretty basic value for most people. It relieves us of the stress of misrepresenting ourselves or lying about things we've done — stress resulting from guilt, remorse, and fear of being found out.

Some of the biggest scandals have resulted not from what was done, but from the cover-up that followed. Do the names Richard Nixon and Enron sound familiar? In the business world, financial misbehaviour is a problem, as is lack of oversight regarding product safety.

Sometimes unintentional contamination occurs in the food industry. In 2008, Michael McCain, CEO of Maple Leaf Foods, responded with forthright honesty and integrity to an outbreak of listeria traced back to one of his plants. He immediately and publicly admitted what had happened and took appropriate steps to correct it, including a hugely expensive recall and shutting down the plant in question. McCain held press conferences, did interviews, and posted an apology on the company web site. The company also ran TV spots and put advertisements in newspapers. This was a smart business decision, to get out ahead of the story and reassure the marketplace. But it was also a rare example of being honest and showing integrity when a mistake was made.

People who own up to mistakes can reduce a lot of stress for themselves — and potentially harmful fallout for other people. They also build trust with others and self-respect for themselves.

Is It Ever OK to Tell a "White Lie"?

When is it OK to tell a "white lie" or a tiny fib? If honesty is one of your sacred principles, is it ever OK to fudge a little bit in order to honour a higher value? I think for all of us the answer is yes. For example, how do you respond when someone asks, "Do you like my new coat?" — and the first thing you want to say is, "That depends on whether or not you can return it."

One of my fondest examples (though not my proudest moment) was when I was visiting my twin sister in Boston in 1969. She had invited her fiancé over for dinner on the night that I arrived. When she served the meal, I noted that the meat was a little overcooked and dried out. In my youthful cheekiness, and because I've always had a close and comfortable relationship with my sister, I thought nothing of observing that the meat was a little dry. Hey, I was just being *honest* (even though my opinion was unsolicited). My sister wisely ignored my comment but turned immediately to her fiancé and asked, "Is the meat too dry?" to which he very tactfully replied, "No, dear, it's fine." He and I had been friends before I introduced him to my sister, so we had a good relationship. But in that moment. I thought, *Are you* serious? *How can you say that?* Clearly, in terms of caring about my sister's feelings, he gave the right response. They've been married ever since!

As important as honesty is as a primary value, there are times in relationships when it's important to consider people's feelings and to show kindness. It also helps us to avoid conflict. I believe this is especially important in families. There is a concept which, in Hebrew, is called *"shalom bayit,"* which means "peace in the home." There are times when maintaining harmony is a higher value than telling the truth, especially when the matter at issue isn't all that important to begin with.

To give another example, anyone who's ever planned a surprise party knows that a certain amount of obfuscation, misrepresentation, and even outright lying is necessary to ensure secrecy. But it's done to serve the greater cause of guaranteeing that deer-in-the-headlights moment when the honoree is greeted with a thunderous, unison chorus of "Surprise!"

4. **Beware of values conflicts involving money.**
A few years ago, a friend told me about a big concert that was taking place in his college town. Its university is famous for many things, among them superb academics, superior sports teams, and excellent cultural programs (music, dance, theatre, etc.). My friend was both a regular supporter of the

arts and a big football fan. He told me about an upcoming Saturday-night concert. I also knew the football team had a big home game that day.

I said, "Boy, it sounds like you're going to have quite a day: the game in the afternoon and the concert in the evening."

He sadly corrected me. "Actually, they're both in the evening."

"What? I've never heard of the football game being played at night. Why would they schedule a game to compete with the concert?"

I'll never forget what he said. "Athletic departments around the country are relinquishing to the television networks their right to control whether games are scheduled during the day or evening. What's clear is that there will be more and more night games. What's also clear is that at this university, football trumps concerts and virtually everything else. It's all about money and television."

When it comes to values conflicts, decisions, and trust, money is often a pivotal issue.

I once had a financial advisor who called me to recommend a new mutual fund. He said, in full disclosure, that it was a fund put together by his own parent company but that he felt it had great value. Because I trusted him, I agreed to invest some money in the fund. Over the next year, it actually *lost* money. I was a bit disappointed, but these things happen, or so I thought.

The final straw came when I later read a newspaper article about the president of his investment firm, who was being charged by the securities regulators for irregular practices. It came out that he was *pushing* his agents to sell that mutual fund. Why? He had put the fund together in order to make quick money for the down payment on a multimillion-dollar home he had just bought. The paper even showed a picture of the mansion in question.

I called my agent and told him that it was now clear that there was a conflict of interest, that what he was promoting wasn't so much high-value to me, the investor, but a way of generating quick money for the company and its president. The financial advisor, a young man whom I had trusted and liked a lot, basically admitted that I had read the situation accurately. It was also clear to me that he was under a lot of pressure from the president to promote this product to all his clients. And though I felt really sorry for him and the position he'd been put in, I told him that he and his company had lost my trust and I was going to move my investments to another organization.

"When People Talk about Money, It's Never about Money"

A friend shared this phrase with me forty years ago and I've observed its truth and wisdom ever since. When you think about it, that dollar in your wallet or the hundred dollars in your bank account has no intrinsic value—until you spend it. Then it's *worth* something. Money is often talked about as currency—which is defined as a "medium of exchange"—in essence, of no value in and of itself.

So why is money so important and central to our lives? It's because it has a whole other level of meaning based on how we think about money. It's fascinating to consider the range of symbolic values we place on money. When I hear couples or families argue about money, I try to discern what they're really fighting about. Whether the parties squabbling about financial issues are spouses, companies, employees, athletes, entertainers, CEOs, or others, the conflicts are about concepts, metaphors, and symbolism—not about dollars, euros, or pesos.

Money may mean the following things to different people:

- **Meeting Basic Needs**
  For many people, money is only for food, clothing, and shelter. It is simply about survival.

- **Freedom, Autonomy, and Independence**
  Money gives people the opportunity to change jobs, leave a bad relationship, or go back to school.

- **Security**
  People put money into savings for the proverbial "rainy day"—an illness, lost job, retirement, and eventually old age. Money in the bank helps folks sleep better at night.

- **Trust, Integrity, and Honesty**
  These qualities are often demonstrated—or betrayed— by the way people handle money. Some examples include how financial advisors and lawyers handle client funds; whether employees and government officials use expense money honestly; and how quickly contractors finish your home renovation after they get your down payment.

- **Responsibility**
  You live within your means; spend money on food for the family rather than on booze or gambling; honour your debts and commitments (for example, paying alimony and child support).

- **Fairness and Justice**
  Workers' salaries, restitution for victims of crime, inheritance decisions, and division of assets are all financial considerations with a broader implication.

- **Control and Power**
  Large amounts of money represent real—or perceived—power to control the lives of others (family members, employees, politicians).

- **Kindness, Caring, and Generosity**
  You can help a disadvantaged relative, neighbour, or others through charitable giving and philanthropy. Some people volunteer time, but many give money as their medium of contributing to the welfare of others.

- **Appreciation and Gratitude**
  This could cover everything from restaurant tips to bonuses at work or holiday gifts to service people.

- **Success, Achievement, and Winning**
  A lot of people measure their success in terms of income and wealth. High-profile examples include entertainers and athletes. Being the highest-paid player may be translated as "I made it. I'm the best."

- **Ego, Self-Esteem, Importance, and Status**
  A lot of conspicuous consumption is based on showing off to the world how superior you are by the way you display or throw around your money. Sadly, many people go into serious debt as a result, just to impress others.

- **Greed and Luxury**

  For some folks no amount of money ever seems to be
  enough. Think of Gordon Gekko's famous "greed is good"
  line in the movie *Wall Street* or our culture's insatiable
  appetite for more/bigger/better.

Whenever you find yourself stressed about money, ask yourself
what you're *really* talking about. What does money mean to *you*
(in general and in any particular situation or context)? Ask yourself whether your stress is about a lack of money or fear of consequences, such as having to sell your
house, or whether there is, in fact, a *values
conflict* underlying your current distress.
For example, I know many people who
have stayed in a job they hated because it
paid well. That's a values conflict. One of
my patients shared his personal philosophy: "Follow your *passion*, not your *pension*."

> "Too many people spend
> money they haven't
> earned to buy things they
> don't want, to impress
> people they don't like."
> —Will Rogers

Values conflicts aren't always internal or "intrapsychic."
They're often interpersonal. So then the question to ask is,
"What does money mean to me and what does it mean to the
other person?" For example, there might be a conflict between
a spouse who wants to save and a spouse who likes to spend.
Or between a business partner who is security-conscious and
a business partner who wants to borrow money to redecorate
the office (possibly from a wish for luxury or to impress the
clients).

Another dimension of the money issue is what parents teach
their children about money. Do they teach them to save and to
give money to charity or to spend every dime that comes into

their hands? In rich families, do they teach their kids to be indus-
trious, to earn money doing part-time jobs — or to just take it
easy and coast, giving them large allow-
ances? As Warren Buffett famously said,
"Leave your children enough money so
that they would feel they could do anything, but not so much that they could do
nothing." Values to live by.

> "Live so that when your
> children think of fairness,
> caring, and integrity, they
> think of you."
> —H. Jackson Brown, Jr.,
> U.S. entrepreneur
> and writer

As important as our principles are to
us individually, there is a wider context in
which to view values conflicts — what we could call our "collective values." Let's explore this domain further.

CHAPTER 21

COLLECTIVE VALUES

Values are not only personal or interpersonal. They're also societal. What do we—as a community, a country, a society—hold to be of highest importance? What are the codes of behaviour, ethics, moral standards, and priorities we prize most?

Dr. Joseph Maddy founded the National Music Camp (NMC) at Interlochen, Michigan, in 1928. It is renowned worldwide and has produced many major stars in the fields of music, theatre, dance, and art. I spent five magical summers there, two as a camper and three as a counsellor and waterfront instructor. They were the most memorable experiences of my youth. However, National Music Camp wasn't just about studying and making great music and art. It was also based on a solid foundation of values.

Because campers came from a wide range of economic backgrounds, from very wealthy homes to very poor families, Dr. Maddy established scholarships based on merit and need. He also introduced a dress code to level out and minimize the economic disparities. The camp uniform consisted of light blue shirts and dark blue corduroy pants for boys, and light blue blouses and dark blue corduroy knickers and knee socks for girls—all supplied by the camp. Everyone dressed alike. Your only fashion statement was the belt you wore or your sweater, sweatshirt, or jacket in cool weather. On their cords, everyone wore a small circular badge that said their name, home city, and state. That was it.

But the dress code didn't just apply to the campers. All the staff and faculty dressed in exactly the same uniforms as the kids. Including Dr. Maddy and his wife. Even guest performers and conductors were given uniforms when they came to camp. Van Cliburn was the most famous pianist in the world in the 1960s, yet, when he came to Interlochen every summer to give a benefit concert, he wore the camp uniform like everyone else. Lyndon Johnson's daughter Luci Baines came to camp in 1964 to narrate a performance of "Peter and the Wolf" with Van Cliburn conducting the orchestra. Her father was the sitting president of the United States, but when she was at camp, she was dressed in knickers and a blouse. It was the great equalizer. The only thing that mattered at NMC was your talent and your character. No one was much interested in what economic stratum you came from. It was a profound values statement.

Joe Maddy also placed a high value on health and physical activity. He chose a beautiful plot of land out in the country, between two lakes near Traverse City, Michigan. Campers were able to swim, canoe, and play tennis and basketball. There were fields in each division to run and play football and soccer. Every camper attended classes for five hours a day, but several hours were also available for recreation and camp activities. And there were concerts every evening given by the campers (orchestras, concert bands, choirs, plays, musicals, dance performances) and some faculty concerts as well. By bedtime, everyone fell asleep pretty fast!

One of the camp highlights every summer was the sixth-week production of a Gilbert and Sullivan operetta. My friend Dude Stephenson was the talented and charismatic director. Operetta was a very popular class. Over two hundred students signed up every summer, most of us in the chorus, with six to eight lead performers who sang the solos, duets, etc. It was incredible fun.

The usual D'Oyly Carte G&S professional operettas had a chorus of twenty to thirty people. Dude had to work with two hundred on a large stage in Kresge Auditorium. The choreography was tricky enough, but Dude had two important principles. He learned everyone's name and he worked out the staging so that, at least once or twice in the show, every chorus member would be in the front row, in full view of the audience (of several thousand people, many of them parents and relatives who had travelled from far and wide to see these marvellous productions). Those two principles came from Dude's system of values: to treat everyone fairly, equally, and respectfully. When he retired after fifty summers, legions of alumni were in the audience for the final performance of his iconic Interlochen operettas to pay him tribute.

Family

Canada is a country of immigrants. Much has been written about the values that newcomers bring to this country. Among the most important are a commitment to hard work, respect for education, and devotion to family. Integrating into the community is also important and is often led by the children who learn the language quickly, get used to the cold and to playing in the snow, participate in local sports—especially ice skating and hockey—and pick up the local lingo, clothing fashions, and culture. They want to fit in, be accepted, and start to feel "at home." However, in many families, preserving their native language and culture is important, and too much assimilation is feared. This can be a source of tension—and stress—between the generations.

Values conflicts can arise when a family member, whether first- or sixth-generation, doesn't like or respect the behaviour of their relatives. Emphasis on money, success, and popularity may not sit well with them. Sarcastic humour, alcohol abuse, or dishonesty might alienate them. Family dynamics are often complicated and values conflicts are often at the root of the dissension my patients tell me about.

Companies

Every organization has a culture, a personality. Some are hard-driving, aggressive, fast-paced, profit-driven, and competitive, with lots of cliques, infighting, guarding information, and keeping secrets. Others are more laid back, relaxed, collaborative, collegial, and concerned about the quality of the work experience for employees, paying attention to things like camaraderie, mentoring, and work-life balance. If you're working in a company that doesn't share your style and values, you're probably experiencing a lot of stress. If you've found a good fit, you're probably not thinking of leaving any time soon.

Company policies dramatically reflect organizational values. We see evidence every day of corporate malfeasance, whether it's a paper mill in Dryden, Ontario, wilfully dumping mercury into a nearby river and polluting local waterways; Mitsubishi purposely falsifying fuel-efficiency data; Wells Fargo creating millions of fake bank accounts for customers; tobacco companies denying the addictive nature of their cigarettes; the NFL suppressing evidence of chronic traumatic encephalopathy (CTE) after years of football players suffering repeated brain concussions — the list goes on.

On the other hand, positive behaviour can give us some encouragement. Costco and Lee Valley Tools have a philosophy of sharing prosperity with their workers, reflected in their practice of fairer wage distribution between employees and top executives.

Dan Price made the news in 2015 when he cut his own one-million-dollar salary so he could give his employees a raise. Price was the founder and CEO of a Seattle processing firm called Gravity Payments. He decided that he wanted his staff members to make at least $70,000 a year within three years. So he started by reducing his own yearly salary to $70,000 and by giving immediate raises to all employees making less than that. Each year would see a gradual increase until they reached the three-year target. CNN reported that Price had been hearing employees talk about the challenges of finding housing and meeting other expenses on their current salary, and he decided there shouldn't be such a big gap between his pay as CEO and that of his workers. He described the raises as a "moral imperative." It could also be called "'putting your money where your mouth is" or honouring your values and putting them into action. In addition, I'd call it visionary leadership and integrity of the highest order.

Society

When we think of societal values, we often think about freedom of speech, freedom of religion, mutual respect, human rights, fairness and justice, compassion and caring for others, health care, education, a living wage, housing and living in safety and dignity. It's hard to dispute any of those enlightened concepts in a civilized, progressive society. But there are different opinions about these issues and how to achieve them.

Political parties are a reflection of the diversity of opinion and values in any society. Whether labelled right, left, or centrist, liberal or conservative, hawk or dove, outward-looking or isolationist, hard-line or compassionate, environmentally progressive or more economically focused, every country has ongoing debates about laws and policies, both internal and international. Controversy keeps politicians, pundits, and the populace busy. Do we build a new pipeline, legalize marijuana, tighten gun laws, expand trade agreements, welcome new immigrants, allow physician-assisted dying, put a tax on carbon, raise the tax rate on the rich, increase the national debt to boost the economy, or rein in spending to balance the books? These are all issues that affect us individually and collectively. So there are tensions about goals and values, but also about what policies should be enacted to pursue those goals.

Honest disagreement is one thing; bad behaviour is another. The field of politics is tainted by numerous scandals and questionable practices that fray our social fabric. Negative campaign advertising and attack ads have been a blight for years. Misrepresenting facts or even outright lying is becoming more common — and, even worse, acceptable. Obstructionism by opposition parties just to make the ruling party look inept and to score cheap political points is an insult to the public. The use of money to buy favour or gain access to lawmakers is another example of the degrading of collective societal values.

The emphasis on money and fund-raising while in office has led to a staggering statistic: a reported 40 percent of the time spent by members of the U.S. Congress is devoted to "call time." This is when they sit on the phone raising money for the next election instead of doing the job they were elected to do. In 2016, the ruling party in Ontario was called out by the media for selling access to cabinet ministers in exchange for large donations to the party in power. There were even fund-raising target goals set for each minister. At least one minister quit politics in disgust at this practice and situation. The values conflict was unacceptable to him. He obviously felt he was not living an authentic life or being true to himself.

Conformity and acceptance by others is another area where values come into play. When I was a teen, lots of kids struggled to get over the coughing and choking of learning to smoke because cigarettes were considered cool and they wanted to fit in. Then they overcame the bitter taste of beer when drinking was the next "in" thing to do.

Dressing to fit in (or stand out) is a major area of conformity as well. This is a different kind of conformity than school (or camp) uniforms that are mandated by institutions to create a level playing field for students. In her book *The Right Words at the Right Time*, Marlo Thomas tells the story of a twelve-year-old black girl living in a working-class neighbourhood in New York City. She was into funky clothes like bell-bottoms, tie-dyed shirts, and torn overalls. One evening a friend didn't want to go to the movies with her unless she changed her clothes. She didn't—so her friend left without her. Her mother heard the conversation and told her she'd have to make a choice in life: to do what everyone else was doing or to follow her own path, daring to be different and risking the judgement and disdain of others. She chose to be her own person. And she still dresses in a nonconformist way.

Here's what Whoopi Goldberg's mother actually said: "You can change your clothes and go ahead and be like everybody else. But if it's not what you want and you're strong enough to take other people's ridicule, then stand by your convictions. You need to know, however, that criticism is what's coming. It's not ever going to be easy because being different never is."

This story isn't just about clothes or conformity. It's also about strength of character. In his important book *The Road to Character*, David Brooks makes a profound distinction between what he calls "resumé virtues" and "eulogy virtues." We live in a society where many people are driven by a credo of "success above all." David Brooks calls it "the culture of the Big Me." In Brooks' distinction, resumé virtues include things like wealth, fame, status, achievements, and accomplishments—things you read in bios or hear about at retirement parties. Eulogy virtues are what you hear about at funerals—the *character* of the individual. Were they kind, generous, brave, honest, loyal, hardworking?

When it comes to individual or collective values, there are often no right or wrong answers. But if your principles are in conflict with those of your family, employer, or community, you will experience more stress. And many people have changed jobs, found new friends, moved out of neighbourhoods, and even left countries when the conflict became too great.

Identifying your own values is the first step to addressing this internal discord. Acting on your values is the second step. More awareness and self-honesty will lead to better choices— and a path to living in harmony with your authentic self.

CHAPTER 22

PRIORITIES

Hockey legend Jean Béliveau was a Canadian icon. Captain of the Montreal Canadiens, he won ten Stanley Cups as a player, seven more as an executive. He was smooth and graceful, the picture of elegance and skill. Equally important, he was respected for his sportsmanship and leadership qualities. But his iconic status had much to do with who he was *off* the ice. He was kind, warm, dignified, and gracious, and he exemplified the word "class." But it was one pivotal decision that may have said more about the man and his values than anything else he ever did.

Béliveau was so highly respected that he was twice offered a seat in the Canadian senate. Both times he declined. He was invited to become Canada's governor general. He graciously turned down that honour as well. His decisions were based on a core value and priority: his family.

He was away from home a lot during his hockey career while his daughter was growing up. She married and had two children of her own. Then, tragically, her husband died. Béliveau passed up the prestigious offers in order to be a constant presence in the raising of his two granddaughters after the death of his son-in-law. He said, "I strongly believe it is my duty to be the father those girls need for the next five years or so." Although he was a proud Quebecker and Canadian, Jean Béliveau put his family ahead of personal honours.

Living your values relates not just to morality and integrity. It also includes your priorities—where you choose to put your time, energy, and attention. Many people espouse one set of values but live in a way that is at odds with those priorities. They say one thing and do another. Their day-to-day lives are incongruent with their underlying values, the things they *say* are important to them. I've seen the stress that this creates in a lot of my patients. They're not living in sync with themselves. The mismatch leads to inner conflict and may create external disharmony as well.

How Well Are *You* Doing at Living in Harmony with Your Authentic Self?

My colleague, psychiatrist Andy Wilson, taught me an exercise that he used with his patients. I adopted it and call it "Assessing Your Values and Priorities." It begins with a list of seven items that I ask patients to rank in order of priority, based on what they value and hold to be most important to them. It looks like this:

What I Value

House/Home

Job

Money

Spouse/Children

Yourself
(health, needs, etc.)

Friends

Family/Relatives

To clarify some terms, "house or home" refers to your abode, the actual physical place where you live. I put "spouse and children" together. I used to separate them, but many patients would just sit there, in a quandary trying to figure out which was more important to them. I combined them so the exercise itself wouldn't *raise* their stress levels! "Family/relatives" relates to extended family members, not immediate kin.

I urge you to do this exercise for yourself. Before actually numbering the items one through seven down the left side of the list, you might want to assign to each of them an A, B, or C, depending on the level of importance you ascribe to them. All of these items may have value for you, but if you can distinguish which are *most* important, it will be easier to do the exercise. The As are the things that are absolutely fundamental to your life; the Bs are important but not as essential; and the Cs are lower on your ladder of priorities, even if only by a small degree. So, say you have two As, three Bs, and two Cs. Then, of the As, decide which is number one and which is number two. Then of the Bs, which would be numbers three, four, and five? Finally, of the Cs, which would be numbers six and seven?

Do this exercise on a sheet of paper, writing the items down the centre as illustrated above and then ordering them one through seven. This will get you thinking about these issues and contemplating your own values.

NOTE: I have an extended version of this exercise that includes a longer list—items such as approval, religion, community, control, security, sex, solitude and tranquility, passions (for example: golf, music, sailing, reading, etc.). You can add one or two items to your list if there's a priority in your life that I have not included.

Now comes the second part of the exercise. This is where the penny drops for most people and the "aha" moment occurs. On the top of the page to the right of your list, write a heading with

the words "How I Live." To the right of the list, again rate the
items with A, B, and C, and then rank them from one to seven.
If I were a fly on the wall observing your behaviour for a week or
two, what would I conclude your values to be? Where do you put
most of your time, your effort, your energy, and your attention?
For example, you may say that family is the most important thing
in your life but spend most of your time at the office. So you may
have ranked "spouse and children" as A1 for what you value — but
in terms of how you *live*, they may show up as a B4 or B5. The
important thing here is to be as objective and honest with yourself
as possible. Where are you *really* putting your time and focus?

A. What I Value	B. How I Live
House/Home	
Job	
Money	
Spouse/Children	
Yourself (health, needs, etc.)	
Friends	
Family/Relatives	

The last part of the exercise is to circle the items with the
greatest discrepancy. Where are the biggest gaps between what
you *value* and how you *live*? These can be viewed as a form of values conflict. Only circle the items where the discrepancy is three
or more numerically. In other words, if something is a one on
one side and a three on the other, that may not be a big gap. But
if it's a one opposed to a four or five, that would be significant.

Now, start to think about how you might bring the two numbers into closer alignment — how to make the way you're living

more congruent with your stated values. I've done this exercise with many patients and helped them to reshape their lives in ways that feel more comfortable and authentic. They start cutting back work hours in evenings and on weekends, and spend more time with their families or getting back into a sport that they gave up years ago. Some people reconsider their work and realize that money is not a high value for them, and yet they've been slaving away to make more of it. Many of my patients left high-pressure/high-paying jobs to work for companies that featured a slower pace and less emphasis on the bottom line. I've seen lawyers leave corporate law firms (with their relentless pressure for billable hours) to work as in-house counsel or to take jobs in the nonprofit sector. Professionals are making different career choices based on the lifestyle they want, not the income they could achieve. A big "aha" for many of my female patients is realizing how much time they spend taking care of their home and family members, and how *little* they devote to taking care of *themselves* (sleep, exercise, time with friends, leisure activities, etc.)

People started to notice the frustration that had been underlying their daily routines or the subtle resentment they'd been feeling as their lives filled up with "shoulds," leaving no time for the things that they enjoyed and that nourished their souls. Mostly, they sensed the stress from these internal conflicts that they had not been fully aware of. Even better, as they made adjustments to bring their behaviour more in line with their priorities, they saw the distress from those conflicts start to melt away.

> "We've all got time for what matters to us. The question is what matters to us?"
> —Salman Rushdie

One of my patients experienced burnout and had to go on stress leave. When she recovered and was preparing to return to her job, she said, "I want to make sure I'm living my values, my authenticity. I wasn't living my values before" (when she was working seventy hours a week and "not meeting my own needs"). And she stood by that commitment, with very positive results. More awareness leads to better choices.

Priorities Change: Different Ages and Stages

It's important to note that our values and priorities change throughout our lives. For example, I played trombone in our local symphony orchestra for nine years before getting married. With a busy medical practice, I was on call or attending meetings one or two evenings a week. Monday-night orchestra rehearsal took me away from my new wife too much. So I took a hiatus for many years. Later, after our kids grew up, I joined the Oakville Wind Orchestra and brought ensemble music back into my life.

Susan and I were both skiers. But we stopped skiing for several years when our kids were small, except for our annual ski vacation in Colorado. When they were old enough to take lessons, we started skiing as a family. Similarly, I cut back on tennis and started running on my lunch hour so I could be home for supper with my family.

How Can You Live More In Sync with Your Priorities?

1. **Clarify your priorities, identify the gaps, and start to make changes.**
   Do the exercise outlined on the previous pages to be clearer about what is important to you and the gaps between what

you value and how you live. Then look for ways to close those gaps, and thus to live a more authentic life.

2. **Rotate your values.**

Roger Mellott's wise saying "identify your values and support them behaviourally" has a corollary: "Rotate your values." Mellott travelled a lot when he was giving stress management presentations. When he was teaching, work was Mellott's primary value. But when he returned home, he focused his time and attention on his family and made *them* his primary value. We all have *several* things that are important to us. We don't have to sacrifice one thing for another if we can figure out a way to *rotate* our values, so that each gets a turn. I think of this as a wheel that keeps turning. I divide the wheel into four sections: work, family, community, and self.

Rotate Your Values

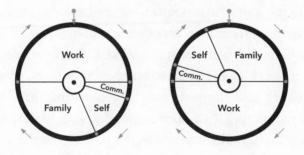

My premise is that if *work* gets a turn at the top (as your primary value), and *family* gets a turn as your primary value, there have to be times when *you* are your primary value. This includes time for nutrition, sleep, and exercise, but it also should include time for leisure, hobbies, friends, entertainment, and relaxation. If the wheel can't turn fully every day, it should at least do so several times a week so that all your priorities get their due. This is a good way to think visually of work-life balance, which is extremely important because work-life balance is not a luxury; it is an antidote to chronic stress.

3. **Combine your values.**
Another way to approach the issue of living your values is to combine them. In a speeded-up, hurried world where most parents also work outside the home, the time-squeeze challenge is a national obsession. Honouring two sets of values at the same time can be a valuable solution.

A creative example of this was shared with me by some friends who loved to play golf. They had two young children, ages six and eight. A round of golf on the weekend takes at least four hours. They had several choices: stop playing golf for a few years; hire a babysitter and go out to hit the links; drag the kids along as spectators and pretend it's a family activity; or actually *include* their children. They rented two golf carts and each parent took a kid. Kids love to ride around on those things. The parents drove off the tees, played the fairways, and chipped onto the greens. But then the kids did the putting. In a normal round of golf, at least half the shots are actually taken with the putter — so the kids had lots of activity on every hole. They felt like they were playing the game and being part of a team. It was a win-win. The children were participants and had fun; and the parents got to play a sport they loved and create enjoyable family time where they could all be together. They combined their values of family, time for leisure, and outdoor activity.

When our two sons were young, most of our nonwork

time was family oriented. We did all kinds of things with our boys, from hiking to swimming, riding bikes to playing games (Uno, Sorry, Pictionary, charades, and marbles were favourites). We even taught them to play poker. My older son would often ask after supper, "What's tonight's activity?" because it was a given that we would play some game together as a family—and it would be a game that we *all* enjoyed (although, occasionally, I'd give in and play Clue, the one game I didn't much relish).

4. **Reach a moment of truth and be willing to take bold action.**
   Many of my patients reached a moment of clarity or had an epiphany about how they had been living their lives only after they experienced a crisis: a serious illness, a marriage breakup, a stress leave from work, or a similar traumatic event. As in *The Monk Who Sold His Ferrari*, Robin Sharma's inspiring megabestseller, some people make a dramatic shift to a new set of values and find physical, mental, emotional, and spiritual peacefulness they didn't have before. Others make similarly big moves to realign their lives with the values they've neglected for a long time. When one of my patients lost her job, her husband quit his and they moved to a quiet town about an hour away, downsized their house and lifestyle, and returned to their roots, where they'd grown up in a less crowded and hurried community. I know people from Canada's Atlantic provinces who have moved home to the Maritimes to get back in sync with a simpler, slower, community-based, and more satisfying way of life that was a better fit than the hustle and bustle of Toronto.

   The shifts and changes don't have to be so dramatic. Many people move out into the country or quit jobs with long hours and relentless pressures, opting for companies that are more laid-back and relaxed. They find that an enjoyable, collegial environment is a better fit for them. Or they downsize their home for a smaller house or condo to simplify their life.

Being clearer about your priorities can reveal a road map to a more congruent, authentic life. There will always be trade-offs. For most people seeking better balance in their lives, decisions often revolve around three things: time, money, and quality of life. There are no right answers, but getting those three things into better balance will lead you to a more harmonious and authentic life.

CHAPTER 23

PREFERENCES

OK, I admit it! As I've gotten older, some things have become apparent to me. I've seen a lot of Shakespeare plays since my teen years, some of them multiple times. But now I find they take too much concentration. It's too much work to follow the dialogue in seventeenth-century English. I also prefer films that don't have subtitles. When I go to the movies, I want to relax and be entertained, not to have to flip back and forth from watching to reading. In addition, I avoid books and movies with a lot of violence and disturbing themes. On a similar note, a therapist friend of mine told me he doesn't go to movies about domestic strife or addictions: "I get enough of that at the office every day. I don't need to watch it on a Saturday night with my popcorn."

In terms of values conflicts, principles and priorities are the big-picture issues, but preferences are a third, albeit less critical, area to explore. Preferences are a smaller subset of priorities. But again, if you make choices that feel more congruent for you, you'll have less conflict, less stress, and more enjoyment in your day-to-day life.

Psychotherapist and author Michele Weiner-Davis uses a very simple formula in her therapy: do more of what works and less of what doesn't. I've adapted it slightly as a prescription for a satisfying life: "Identify the things you enjoy and do more of them. Identify the things you don't enjoy and do less of them." Could it be any simpler? Of course, we can't live only according to our whims and wants. There may be time or financial limitations. You might love live theatre, but it's a lot more expensive than going to the movies. There are also interpersonal considerations. We often make compromises with our families and friends. Tim Allen (as Tim Taylor on *Home Improvement*) told his wife, Jill, he'd go to the opera with her—which he cynically called "death by singing"—if she'd go to the monster truck rally with him (or maybe it was a wrestling match). One person might want to go dancing on a Saturday night while the other might prefer a quiet dinner with friends.

I once heard a phrase that I've used many times with my patients and in my own life: "Tell the truth about..." Even if only to *yourself*, be candid and honest—and don't judge yourself for your preferences. They are what they are. It can be the truth about activities you enjoy or don't like, people you love being around and those you'd rather avoid, your preferences in music or reading material. I was given a complimentary membership at a fitness club years ago (when I served on their advisory board). One of the trainers designed an exercise program for me, combining aerobics and weight training. I went four times. The last straw came on a gorgeous Saturday morning in September. I was slugging away indoors while gazing longingly at the sunny day outside. I finally admitted to myself that I prefer outdoor activities. I had been a runner for twenty years and ran outside twelve months a year. I played touch football in the snow every winter in my twenties and thirties and loved it. Working out at a gym wasn't my thing. It's a small issue in the whole scheme of things, but it illustrates a values conflict in this specific area. When I do what I like to do, I not only enjoy it more, but I'm much more motivated to do it. A lot of people avoid exercise because they don't enjoy the activity they've chosen. If you find walking boring, ride your bike or play squash. But don't keep doing something you find unpleasant.

Another example is reading preferences. I gave a friend a book for his birthday that I thought he'd enjoy. He was honest enough to tell me that the topic wasn't of great interest to him — but he *loved* reading about history. Some people read only non-fiction. They feel that novels are a waste of time. You might gravitate toward romance stories or light, humorous fare, while others prefer self-help or something with a message. Another thing: if a book hasn't hooked me in fifty or a hundred pages, I stop reading and start something else. I used to think I had to finish a book once I'd started. The pivotal moment for me came on a vacation some years ago. I was plodding through a book, waiting for it to finally come alive or redeem itself in some way. It never did. Now I prefer books that I can't put down and luckily there are lots of them.

Same with individual preferences in TV shows and movies. Do you favour drama? Biographies? Documentaries? Some folks like watching a movie two or three times; for others, once is enough even if they enjoyed it. (Between *The Sound of Music* and *Mary Poppins*, my brother holds the record for rerun viewing!)

Musical tastes vary as well. Why listen to rap when you prefer classical? For some people early rock 'n' roll is heaven, while others want punk or heavy metal. If country and western is your thing, load up on it. I'm a classical/rock 'n' roll/folk guy. You may be into New Age. Identify your preferences and invite more of them into your life. Just be honest and connect with your authentic self.

What kind of sports do you prefer — for you or for your kids? What do you value when playing games? Friendly competition or winning? I play doubles tennis with a group of guys who are a perfect fit for me. We all play hard, going after every ball and every point — and no one cares who wins. The banter between points just adds to the fun. I won't play golf with people who take the game too seriously—but in truth they probably wouldn't want to play with *me*. When it comes to children's sports, where do you want the focus to be? And where do *they* want it to be? Exercising, learning skills, having fun, and working as a team? Or winning at all costs, getting the maximum amount of playing time, and being the star? If you (or your child) prefer one thing but get the other, chances are you won't be enjoying yourself much. A lot of kids drop out of team sports because of the mismatch between what they experience and what they enjoy.

Dinner parties are another area where conflicts may arise between your preferred evening and the kind you often spend. For some, their comfort zone is small gatherings of four to six people. Others don't think it's a party unless there are ten to twelve people seated at a large table with three or four conversations going at once. Some people like serious, lively, even contentious discussion or debate, with passionate points of view being aired (which might be the reason politics was invented!). Others prefer lighter topics, harmonious exchanges, and lots of laughs.

Food is a big part of our lives. We need to eat for sustenance, but culinary tastes vary widely. When we eat fajitas, a family favourite, we have two kinds of salsa on the table: mild for me and my wife, spicy hot for our kids—in fact, the hotter the better for them. Poached eggs make me gag—I like my eggs fried like shoe leather. Different strokes and all that. If you're adventurous, you'll want to check out all the new exotic restaurants. Others will stay with more familiar cuisine when they eat out. Go for whatever lights up your taste buds. But also be willing to push yourself outside of your comfort zone to explore other possibilities.

I'm purposely citing mundane examples to illustrate that preferences can be small and specific but can still make a difference in how you live your life. We make choices all day long, big choices and little choices. We might as well make decisions that please us and enrich our lives, that are more congruent with who we really are. Identify your values and, as much as possible, give yourself permission to pursue them. Increased awareness and better choices are the keys to living a more authentic life.

LIVING YOUR PASSIONS
VS.
FOLLOWING OTHER PATHS

CHAPTER 24

PASSIONS AND DREAMS: SIGNPOSTS ON LIFE'S JOURNEY?

Carol was giving me a tour of her high school. She was the principal and I was shadowing her for a morning to prepare for a seminar she'd asked me to give. As she showed me around the school, I looked around in wonder. I said,

> "When your heart speaks, take good notes."
> —Judith Campbell

"Carol, let's stop for a minute. I so envy you. This is the life *I* wanted to have. I always wanted to be a teacher, but I got talked out of it by my guidance teacher."

She stopped abruptly, as if she'd walked into a wall. "You're kidding," she said. "I wanted to be a doctor—but I got talked out of it by *my* guidance teacher!"

Here's how my story unfolded. In April of my senior year in high school, the guidance teacher called me in for a chat. "Are you planning to go to university?"

"Yes."

"Well, you need to apply soon."

"I guess so."

"What would you like to do?"

"I want to be a teacher."

"Have you ever thought about medicine?"

(He might just as well have asked if I wanted to be an astronaut or a lounge singer!)

"No, I want to be a teacher."

"I think you'd make a very good doctor."

What was this man not hearing? I'd been tutoring younger students in math and science for five years, taught swimming at summer camp, stood in for absent teachers as a school prefect, and was a student teacher for two years at my religious school. I *loved* teaching. I *knew* I loved teaching. And I felt I was good at it.

He continued, "Why don't you go down and talk to the dean of the medical school?"

I thought, *Whatever for? This is crazy. Why would I waste the dean's time? What would I say to him?*

A week later, for reasons I still can't fathom, I put on a shirt, tie, and jacket, rode the streetcar to the University of Toronto Medical Building, and met with Dean MacFarlane. I don't remember much of the conversation except my asking him, "How do you know if you want to be a doctor if you're not sure?" (I guess I was being polite. I should have said, "—if you haven't the slightest interest in medicine?") I added, "I have friends who've known they want to be a doctor since they were ten."

His answer was interesting although not relevant to me. "I'd rather have someone decide to be a doctor at age eighteen for the right reasons than at age ten for the wrong reasons."

I left the meeting confused and conflicted.

I talked it over at home and got a good suggestion from my older brother. "If you're not sure about what course to take, why don't you start pre-med and if you don't like it, switch into arts or sciences and finish a bachelor's degree? But if you *do* like it, you'll save yourself a year getting into medicine." (In those days, you could enter medical school after two years of pre-med instead of getting a three- or four-year undergraduate degree first.) It sounded reasonable so I took his advice.

That spring I got an application for pre-med at U of T, took it with me to the summer camp where I was working—and promptly forgot about it. In early August, it suddenly dawned on me that I hadn't sent the application. I dug it out and saw that the deadline was only days off and I was three hundred miles away. That afternoon, I sat on my bunk and filled out the eight pages of questions. (The best was, "Why do you want to be a doctor?" I had to call on all my creative writing skills to come up with some kind of an answer to that one.)

I finished the application only to find that they needed a picture to accompany the document. I didn't have a photo and there wasn't time to get one sent up from Toronto. Then I had a brain wave. One of my campers had a new Polaroid camera that produced an instant photograph. I asked him to take a picture of me. On this hot, muggy day, I put on the shirt, tie, and jacket I'd brought with me for the final banquet. He snapped a picture, including my shorts and bare feet. I then cropped it, slapped it on the application, and threw it into the mail. My level of enthusiasm was nonexistent.

When I got home in late August, I found my acceptance letter in the mail. It said to call right away to reserve my spot in the class or it would be offered to the next person on the list. Days went by. Each night my brother asked if I'd called the university and I said no. Finally, on about day four, *he* phoned and said, "This is David Posen. I'll be there." And that's how I started my medical education.

How many signals did I need to tell me this was not what I wanted? Could I have been any more indifferent? These are the telltale signs we all should notice and heed as we make decisions in life. Sometimes your gut gives you very clear messages. Even though I was only eighteen, I was not a passive kid. I don't know why I didn't have the courage to stand up and declare myself.

I started pre-med in September with absolutely no enthusiasm. It was OK. At times it was interesting, but I wasn't really hooked on the sciences anymore. I got another strong clue that I might be in the wrong place when my favourite subjects were English, philosophy, and psychology, but by then I was making friends in the class and getting used to being in the medical faculty.

The good news is that I came to enjoy the study of medicine. Med school itself was fascinating and challenging, and becoming a doctor afforded me amazing experiences (especially practising in the Canadian Arctic and the Middle East) and led to many lifelong friendships. As I look back, I have no regrets — especially because I finally found my way back to teaching and the work I'd always loved.

Today, I'm in my third career. I was a family doctor for seventeen years before doing stress and lifestyle counselling full-time for five years. Then I added public speaking and writing to my professional activities. I still see patients, but most of my work is preparing and giving lectures and seminars. I also write books on stress mastery, work-life balance, resilience, and workplace stress. And I've never enjoyed my work so much. I love what I do. I wake up every day with a sense of anticipation and enthusiasm that I didn't have earlier in my career. And the irony is that, after a thirty-year odyssey, I'm doing what I always knew in my heart that I wanted to do. I'm a teacher. Instead of teaching high school students about English and history — my original plan — I'm teaching adults about stress and health issues. But I'm teaching. It's the right fit. I feel like I'm home.

SYD'S STORY

Syd asked if he could join me for breakfast in the hotel dining room of a small farming town in western Canada. I was about to present a seminar at an agricultural conference and he wanted to make a suggestion for my talk. "Tell them to follow their dreams." Then he told me his story.

He was a third-generation farmer working with his father. The plan was that he would eventually take over the business, which was a mixed-grain and cattle farm. When his father was sixty-four, he asked Syd what he was going to do with the farm after he took it over.

Syd said, "I don't want to tell you."

His father said, "I'm curious to know."

"I'd rather not tell you."

"Well, I really want to know."

"OK, Dad, I'll tell you. I'm going to turn it into a cattle farm. All cattle. I think we're wasting too much time and effort and land on the grain side, and we can't fully develop the cattle side the way I'd like to."

"Have you done the pencil work? Have you run the numbers? Do you think you can make it work?"

"Yes, I've worked it out and I'm sure I can make it go."

His father looked at him and said, "Then let's do it *now*!"

"What?"

"That's what *I've* always wanted to do too. But I never thought it would work. I never thought I could make enough of a living. If you think it'll work, don't wait till I die. Let's do it *now*."

Syd continued the story. "The next year we plowed all the crops under and turned the land into pasture and just raised cattle. My father woke up every day with a smile on his face from that day on. He lived on the farm and was happy till the day he died at the age of eighty-six."

He concluded by saying, "Tell them to have a dream and to follow that dream instead of doing what you think is expected or doing what other people want you to. Decide what you want to do and then go for it."

Syd made a tremendously successful business out of his dream. And he feels happy and fulfilled.

Passion for some activity or interest could be called the spice of life. It's what you're drawn to, what totally engages you, what you want to do above all else. But it's also what gives your life colour, excitement, and pleasure. Wouldn't it be nice if you could find that in your work?

When and Why Work Doesn't Work

My interest in job satisfaction—and dissatisfaction—stems from my observation that, for so many of my patients, disliking their work is the major cause of their stress. Jobs can be stressful for many reasons: overload, long hours, deadlines, lack of resources, fast pace, jerk bosses, demanding clients, conflict with coworkers, the feeling of not being capable, a lack of confidence, etc. But what if you just dislike the work itself? Or find it boring and unfulfilling? Or even hate it? The very nature of the job can be the problem. Perhaps it doesn't resonate for you. Or maybe it's just a bad fit.

Many of my patients over the years have been unhappy in

their work. I sometimes ask what led them to their occupation and what keeps them there.

- One patient drifted into something because of circumstance. His friend worked at a local factory. A position opened up and his pal suggested he check it out. With no other plans at the time, he applied and got the job.

- Another dropped out of school to take over the family business when his father died.

- One young woman had to get a job out of high school because there was no money for college, even though she'd wanted to become a nurse.

- Another woman found work at a local business because that was all that was available in her small town.

- An aspiring medical student applied to several medical schools but wasn't accepted. He would have made a wonderful doctor. Instead, he reluctantly decided to get a business degree, thus giving up on his dream.

- A highly successful professional had been pushed into his field by his father, who was in the same profession. He was a very creative guy who had lots of ideas he wanted to pursue as an entrepreneur, but he was reluctant to give up his six-figure income and expensive lifestyle. Sometimes it can be hard to break out of those "golden handcuffs."

- Several of my classmates in medical school had parents who were doctors. One told me years later that he'd wanted to be an engineer. His father told him, "You can do anything you want—*after* you get your MD."

- Someone who taught dental students shared this observation with me. "I met a lot of stressed-out kids whose families had decided for them at some early age that they would be a dentist. So you have these kids who come in and their entire family has pooled together all their resources to put one child through dental school. And so this huge pressure sits on them. And they may have no aptitude for the actual requirements (for example, mechanical three-dimensional problem-solving skills or fine motor co-ordination), even though they may have straight As in the academic subjects. They're in denial about who they are, about what they want. It's an anxiety problem. It's a stress problem. Somebody else chose this for them."

Work is one of what I call the "Big Three" sources of stress, along with relationships and money. A 2013 survey showed that 47 percent of working Canadians said their work and workplace was the most stressful part of their life. Too many people reluctantly drag themselves to a job every day because they have to earn a living. They wait for the weekend to find some enjoyment. Many of these people have no choice — or *feel* they have no choice. But what if they *did* have a choice?

> "We act as though comfort and luxury were the chief requirements of life, when all that we need to make us really happy is something to be enthusiastic about."
> —Charles Kingsley, English author and clergyman

Every job is going to include *some* stress. As Malcolm Forbes said, "If you have a job without aggravation, you don't have a job." If you love what you're doing, you handle it. It's part of the deal. But if you fundamentally dislike what you're doing, the stress becomes magnified and can become intolerable. This is what got me interested in this whole topic. I've had jobs where I dreaded going to work. I'd have a knot in my stomach and a headache most days. I've also had jobs where I couldn't wait to get at it, where I loved what I was doing. Passion for my work made all the difference.

My formula for following your passion(s) has three parts:

- Acknowledge them if they're clear to you.

- Discover them over time, through experience.

- Pursue them as best you can.

So let's explore the issue of passion and career choice. We'll meet three groups of people: those who followed their passion early, those who switched later on, and those who didn't or couldn't combine passion with their work.

CHAPTER 25

THE LUCKY ONES

Rob's Story: Childhood Passion, Adult Career

Rob was a sportscaster. Mind you, he had a limited audience—mostly his intrigued parents and amused neighbours. He was seven years old.

Young Rob would go out into the backyard and pretend to be the Toronto Blue Jays, imitating every player down to the last detail—whether they threw left-handed, their exact batting stance, and so on. All Rob wanted to do was describe what he was seeing, mimicking the play-by-play announcers he'd heard on radio and TV.

> "Growing up, if hockey wasn't my sole focus at any given time, it was close. It was a way of life for me from as far back as I can remember." —Gordie Howe

When he was nine, Rob corralled his younger brother to come out to the yard to play with him. Rob would be the Blue Jays and little brother would be the other team. (Kid brothers will follow older ones anywhere!) And as they played the game, using a tennis ball and a light wooden bat, Rob would be talking about what was going on. His attention to detail was so faithful that he used real players and their batting averages. They'd even start each game by standing and singing the national anthems.

As an eight-year-old, Rob would listen to the games on the radio and say, "How do I get to be that guy? I want to be that guy." But he realized, even at that age, that there can't be many of "those guys." He wondered, even back then, how he could fit into a career such as broadcasting, how he could finagle his way into the "fraternity." And while his little brother just enjoyed hitting the ball, Rob's greatest joy was talking about the games, describing the action. In the winter, it was ball hockey on the driveway, wearing his Leafs jersey, and pretending to be different players, all the while broadcasting the game as he was playing it.

As he got older, Rob imagined himself in the press box, talking about the action and sharing the game with people through his words. By age nine, he couldn't wait till he got older and could make this a career. He said, "It's all I want to do. It's about broadcasting, interacting through a microphone and phone calls, interacting with the audience and sharing the passion, but also being able to bring them information they didn't know about. It's a lot of fun to be a bit of a conduit, to be in the middle of it."

The backyard baseball and driveway hockey "broadcasts" ended when Rob was eleven. In high school he was an all-around athlete, playing several sports and being more of a participant than an observer, but he took some media-related courses where he could. He went on to a two-year radio program at a community college—which included running the college radio station. "Every day you had an opportunity to hone your craft and try different things. That was really the point where I knew I loved it and I could do it. I was taught how to do it and then given the opportunity to try it."

After college, he started with entry-level jobs in the media industry, working his way into broadcasting sports at a major-league level and loving every minute of it. He studied statistics and injury reports, did his prep work, went to the stadium every day, talked to the players and coaches, and worked hard. Although he wasn't the play-by-play announcer, he was on air before and after every game and during intermissions, and was often invited to be a guest on other sportscasters' shows to talk about his team. He described his success as "a culmination of a lot of hard work, at times awkward hours, but I don't look at it that way because I love what I do so much."

He added, "I make a comfortable living, but you're not going to get rich in this business. You're doing it for the passion. It's been a decade of grinding it out. The message I would have is: my business, especially in the early days, is about passion. In this business, if you're successful at it and it's a passion for you, it's not work. I have no regrets about where I'm at right now. I'm very happy with it. Deep down I always knew what it was I wanted to do and I always knew it would work out."

Shelley's Story: Parallel Careers — The Best of Both Worlds

Shelley Posen is a recently retired curator from the Canadian Museum of History in Ottawa. He is also a professional folk singer, accomplished songwriter, and wonderful storyteller. Full disclosure: Shelley is also my warm, funny, bright, immensely talented first cousin and friend.

Shelley's intertwined passions started early. His mother was the musical influence. She was always singing and playing records, and they had a piano. His father took him to a Pete Seeger concert when he was twelve and a spark was lit. Shelley thought, *This is it! I want to learn to do that.* So he got Pete's records. But he was also listening to all the music on the radio and was passionate about the Everly Brothers, rock 'n' roll, and doo wop, "sponging it in, absorbing it all."

But Shelley's parents gave him a sense of needing something to fall back on, that he couldn't just be a musician, and that education was important. So he got an English degree while singing in the university choir and performing at local folk music festivals on banjo and guitar. "I was OK at English litera- ture, but it wasn't my passion. Folklore was my passion. I wanted to know about folk song." When he found out you could get a Ph.D. in folklore, he began doing graduate work at Memorial University in Newfoundland.

"I came to folklore through folk music. I went to Memorial to learn more about folk songs and I found folklore. I began to see folklore as a key to understanding the world. It was a real revelation. Memorial University was where I became a folklor- ist." A key moment of direction came when he was stopped in the hall by his department head, who gave him some valuable feedback and advice. "Why are you bothering with all of this theory stuff? You are a field-worker. You are a collector. You go out there and you find out about things. You can talk to people and you can bring back songs. You can bring back the informa- tion. That's what you do well." Sometimes others see us better than we see ourselves.

"I knew I made the right choice whenever I was doing field- work. And the world started to come together, to make sense, where I could see things that other people didn't, or I could see patterns or purposes, or understand why certain things were happening. Those were the magic moments that still give me a sense of satisfaction."

Shelley went on to do a Ph.D. at the University of Pennsylvania. He did fieldwork in Chapleau, Ontario, for eighteen months, then returned to Philadelphia to write his thesis. It was there that he met a fellow folklorist—his future wife—and the two of them were hired to do a folklore project in Brooklyn, which they did for three years. "Instead of just looking at song, I was looking at everything. That's where I got the breadth that I needed for what I was going to do after." His passion, education, and experience were all meshing together.

Although those early years were difficult financially, Shelley learned his craft as he went from project to project. And he found he enjoyed going from one project to another. He didn't want to be an academic. He realized that "my personality and my proclivities were more toward working with the public, finding out detailed things about stuff, and then making what I'd learned available to nonspecialists. That's what I do, and I do it well. I love working with photographers and videographers and being the content guy, the guy who knows the stuff, and then trying to figure out the creative ways of putting it all across.

"I'm constantly looking for things to be passionate about. In music, I've gone from genre to genre. I went from Jewish music to English folk music, from bluegrass to country music, from Sacred Harp to English Renaissance choral music—the list keeps on going. And that has happened in folklore as well. I need to have passions. I'm a serial, monogamous passion follower."

Shelley moved to Ottawa and gradually got into the folk music world there. Ian Robb, an old friend from the Toronto scene, was also in Ottawa and invited him to sing on an album he was recording. Shelley appeared as a session musician on the album, which got him back into music and the Ottawa folk community. Shelley and Ian later met a woman named Ann Downey, and the three of them formed a folk trio called Finest Kind. They sang together for twenty-four years, recording five albums and performing professionally in Canada, the U.S., and the U.K.

Shelley noted something very important. "The beauty of it, the part of my luck, is that the folk music and folklore were compatible with each other. What I was learning in one I was able to feed into the other, in both directions. My life was very integrated."

He later started writing little songs for children's entertainers Sharon, Lois & Bram. Shelley found that he loved to write songs on commission. But he expanded his creative repertoire substantially, eventually writing and recording four solo albums on his own.

"Those same kind of moments come when I find the right word or I get the right piece of information for a project I've been trying to put through—you know, the adrenalin turns into whatever endorphins they're supposed to, and I feel 'This was a good day; this is what I should be doing.'"

Shelley used the word "luck" about three times in our conversation and said that was clearly also a piece of his journey and success. "I've met so many people who are doing something that they love to do and I ask them, 'How'd you do this?' and they say, 'Well, you know I was an engineer, then X happened and Y happened.'"

He summed it up this way: "You know, show-business people talk about 'breaks.' Luck does have a lot to do with it. But you have the talent, hopefully, and your arm has to be out to grab the ring as it goes by. And hopefully you have a good enough aim and the strength to get it and you're on the right horse."

> "Ah, but a man's reach should exceed his grasp, Or what's a heaven for?"
> — Robert Browning

Some people are fortunate. They know what they want to do from an early age and develop a love affair with it. I'm always interested in people who followed their passions when choosing a career or profession. I've worked with countless doctors who love their work: interacting with patients, problem solving, diagnostic dilemmas, and therapeutic challenges — not to mention the satisfaction of curing illness, relieving suffering, and comforting patients and their families. It's gratifying on several levels and for many it feels more like a calling than an occupation.

I know artists, journalists, mathematicians, firefighters, interior decorators, pilots, athletes, nurses, musicians, salespeople, entrepreneurs, and others who just love what they do. Some of them faced daunting odds to succeed in their careers, but they persisted because they couldn't imagine doing anything else. Actors go to endless auditions; stand-up comics ply their trade in small comedy clubs for years, hoping for a big break but still relishing being part of the scene. Authors and songwriters have told me they can't *not* write — it's in their bones, their soul. I may be waxing rhapsodic at the romance of it all, but, notwithstanding the struggles and sacrifice, that's how many people feel.

So what about everybody else? What if you're not among the fortunate folks who blend their passions with their work? What if you don't know what your passion is? According to career consultant Peter Caven, we don't have a clear understanding of ourselves until we're in our thirties. Research shows only about 4 percent of university graduates have any "passion" that is career-related and actionable. What to do then? Let's explore this common situation if you're not one of the lucky few.

CHAPTER 26

HOW DO YOU FIND OR DISCOVER YOUR PASSIONS?

Passions often develop only over time and with experience.

Jacob got a summer job working for a landscaping company. It was entry level, mostly cutting grass, trimming bushes, and raking flowerbeds. He enjoyed the job, discovering that he really liked physical work and being outdoors. After high school, the job became full-time. Then he started to build on that foundation. He took courses in horticulture, learning about flowers and trees. Then he learned more about gardens, including soil conditions, irrigation, what to plant where according to climate, rainfall, and sunlight. Not stopping there, he took courses in landscape architecture, combining artistry and aesthetics with the science he'd learned. As he got more experienced, he started his own landscaping business, developing a career that was both stimulating and satisfying. He found his passion in gradual stages, beginning with a humble seasonal job that he'd taken in high school to earn some pocket money.

What if you don't know what your passions are and have never envisioned an ideal job? After all, throughout history, work was something you did out of necessity, not for enjoyment. You can start by exploring things about yourself and your preferences. What would an enticing job look like to you? What would be some of the ingredients or criteria? I put this question to a disillusioned corporate manager in his fifties. I'll never forget his answer: "It would have to have a golf course in it." Golf was his main passion, but, until that moment, he'd never considered the possibility of creating a job or career around golf and golf courses. He also said, "It would have to include some outdoor activity, not being tied to an office and a desk." Another helpful clue.

Ask yourself what features an exciting job would have for you. Start with "I want to work with—" and then fill in the blank with whatever you can think of: people, ideas, books, my hands, the outdoors, nature, children, numbers, a small team. I want to help people. I want routine and structure. I want variety and for every day to be different. I want work that involves travel. I want to work for a cutting-edge start-up. I want to be self-employed. Begin to map out some parameters as a starting point. Then flesh it out with more details. For example, you might have a strong interest in theatre or film. The next question is whether you want to be a performer, a script writer, a director, or a backstage person on the technical side (costumes, props, lighting, etc.). Find someone to help you with this—an experienced friend, an older relative, a teacher who knows you, or a professional career counsellor.

Drawing on early experience, especially part-time jobs as a kid, might also give you a sense of what you *don't* want to do. One young man worked in retail and in a call centre and roundly disliked both. I sold water coolers and plastic dental mirrors door-to-door just long enough to find out that sales was not my happy place. The more things you try, the more the process of elimination can help you to zero in on what would be a good fit for you.

The eminent philosopher and author Joseph Campbell said, "Follow your bliss." But how do you identify what that is? Here are some questions to help you.

What Do You Do When You Do What You *Like* to Do?

What are the interests, hobbies, and activities that really ring your chimes? What do you find yourself doing when you have time to do whatever you want? What do you gravitate toward, often without realizing it or seeing a pattern? Amy had a passion for baking. Even though she got a university degree in fine arts and found work in the nonprofit sector, it really didn't excite her. What she really loved was baking cakes and cookies on the weekends. Finally it occurred to her that she might be able to turn that passion into a job. She took the plunge when she found a position in a small baking business in her neighbourhood. She found her niche. It allowed her to do what she loves, hone and expand her culinary skills, and as a bonus gave her an outlet for her artistic flair. She's been happy ever since. More awareness led to a better choice.

- Do you tinker with motors? That's how many mechanics got started.

- Do you draw in a sketchbook? Many painters, graphic artists, and illustrators found they not only loved doing this but that they were good at it.

- Do you play around with computers? Lots of computer geeks and enthusiasts gravitate to IT jobs or work with tech companies. I know two young men who began with a fascination for video games and now design and create games for a living.

- Do you love browsing the Internet? A career in research might await you.

- Do you write poetry or short stories? A literary career might be great for you, either as an author, editor, or publisher.

- Do you strum a guitar? Music performance or teaching might be a career path to pursue.

- Do you enjoy puttering around the house and fixing things? That could be a signal for a career in construction, contracting, or a renovation business.

- Are you a sports nut who reads the baseball box scores before checking out the news section of the paper? Maybe you can get into sportswriting or a job with a local team.

- Are you a political junkie or newshound who's glued to the Sunday-morning current affairs shows? Journalism might be an avenue to pursue.

- Do you love reading about computer science and technology? Computer sales or service might be for you.

- Do you have a thing for movies? That's a big industry with lots of jobs to look into. Or you might start a movie review blog and catch on with some news outlet.

- Is downhill skiing an adrenalin rush for you? I know several people who went out to the Rockies to teach skiing or work at ski resorts when they were young. They loved the adventure and the sport and found a way to make a living from it. One guy stayed out west and opened a ski shop when his days on the slopes ended.

What kinds of activities and pursuits really light you up? These are helpful clues to some of your passions. Wouldn't it be great to think there might be a career opportunity in there?

What Kinds of Activities Did You Love Doing in the Past?

Patients often tell me about things they used to do but gave up somewhere along the way. If I had a nickel for every person who's told me they used to fish or play tennis or go canoeing or build model airplanes or travel or do scrapbooking or play trumpet or read novels or listen to opera, I could probably fund a vacation. I call these "forgotten or neglected pleasures." One woman was an accomplished pianist who hadn't played in years. Another had been an avid seamstress, making clothes for her family and friends, but hadn't opened her sewing box in a decade. Not all of these passions will lead to a career, but maybe one of them could.

What Clues or Feedback Can You Get from Other People?

Back in 1992, I read a new book called *Your Money or Your Life*, which deservedly became a classic. It encouraged readers to "take a few moments now to reflect upon your dreams" and answer some questions. I was at the breakfast table with my wife and I said, "The book wants me to stop reading and identify my passions."

She said, insightfully, "Oh, for you, that's easy."

"What do you mean?" I thought she'd say "sports," a lifelong passion of mine.

"You love to learn." I was stunned by the simplicity and pinpoint accuracy of her observation.

"But to learn for what purpose? You mean to learn in order to *teach*?"

"No, you love to learn just to *learn*."

It was a lightbulb moment. I would never have come up with that insight on my own, but to my perceptive wife, it was perfectly clear. I'm a constant reader, I listen to public radio, and I'm always curious and fascinated by new knowledge. Yes, I love to gain information so I can teach others, but it has intrinsic pleasure as well. Learning is its own reward.

I realized that, in addition to my own ideas, I'm also in the "learning and sharing" business. That's what I'm really doing with my patients and my seminars. But it's also what I'm really about, it's part of my essence, what I'm drawn to and what resonates in the deepest part of me. When I learn some new piece of information, the first thing I want to do is tell it to someone. It's like your first impulse when you hear a new joke. My wife helped me to understand another dimension of my life-long love affair with teaching: my passion for learning.

> "Chase the dream but love the journey."
> — Rosie MacLennan, 2016 Olympic trampoline champion

Sometimes we can't see what's obvious to people who know us well. Just as my wife so clearly saw my passion, your family, friends, and work colleagues can probably give you some helpful clues. Ask them when they think you're at your best; when you're strongest; when you're happiest. Their observations might help—and even surprise you!

Ron Coupland was a therapist in Oakville when I arrived in 1971. I referred patients to him and he became a mentor— and later a close friend. We shared many dinners together, and one evening I told him my story about wanting to be a teacher instead of a doctor. As I related my dream of teaching English and history, Ron noted that I became quite animated and energized. He gave me a serious look and asked, "Why don't you pursue that now?" I was a busy GP in my thirties. I hemmed and hawed, and said I'd have to go back to school for several years, give up my practice and income, etc. He then said something I'll never forget: "Anything that can put that look on your face is something I wouldn't ignore!" While I couldn't see how I could start over (or more accurately, didn't have the *courage* to start over), the thought stayed with me. It found its expression in my career change at age forty-two when I gave up family medicine and became a teacher of stress management. I've never been happier in my work.

KRIS'S STORY

Kris was born into a military family and was headed for a military career himself. He was also a Rhodes scholar who studied for a year at Oxford University. One day, still in uniform, he was at a concert at the Grand Ole Opry and met Johnny Cash backstage. "Just shaking his hand was electric. I'm sure that's when I decided I'm not going back to the army." Kris moved to Nashville to pursue his passion for music, and took an entry-level job in a recording studio. In the evenings, he hung out with the musicians and wrote songs. Those were very happy years for him. "I never felt I was in the wrong place." But his folks were not pleased. "I was disowned by my parents for following my dream." Ironically, their rejection of Kris's career choice was liberating. "It wasn't easy, but in a sense, it was a lucky thing to happen because I had nothing else to lose then. I had nothing left to do but just enjoy the life that I was leading. And I was in heaven even though I wasn't making any money as a writer. I never ever regretted making that move."

Kris's passion led him to follow his dream and, after five years of struggle, he never looked back. He penned some of the best lyrics, composed some of the best tunes, and recorded some of the best songs in the history of country and folk music. He followed his passion and enjoyed the *journey* as well as the success that resulted. His full name is Kris Kristofferson, an icon of American popular music.

Other Questions to Ask Yourself

- What do you resent not having more time for?

- What do you daydream and fantasize about doing?

- What would you like to be doing, or doing *more* of, if you had more time?

- What's on your "someday, when I retire . . ." bucket list?

- What would you want to do if you had more money? Or if money wasn't an issue?

- What would you like to do even if you weren't *paid* for it?

ALEX'S STORY

Alex was a university graduate in his early twenties when his father died. After his father passed away, Alex worked for a couple of years at his office, a job he disliked. "I real-ized that I needed to do something that I loved."

One day Alex said to a friend, "I really want a job in sports." To which his friend replied, "I'm sick of you saying it. Do it already." He had seen the Montreal Expos play, an experience that reignited a passion for baseball that had been developed years earlier. So Alex decided to pursue a career in the game. With his degree in economics, he was interested in the business end of baseball, so Alex started calling major league teams for a job. He finally got to speak to the general manager of the Expos. "I said I would work for free doing something I love." He even paid the $1,000 to go to scout school. Alex was twenty-three years old.

He later met someone who worked for the Toronto Blue Jays and moved from Montreal to join their front office. It had taken him two years to get paid. But he persevered, moving up the ladder to eventually become the team's general manager in 2009. In 2015, the Jays made the playoffs and Alex Anthopoulos was voted Major League Baseball's General Manger of the Year by his peers.

Alex concluded: "It's so critical to do something that you love."

Here's an instructive story told to me by a friend:
"I once worked on a boat for a couple of weeks while I was at university, taking a sailboat through the locks from Lake Ontario to Lake Erie. And there was a guy onboard the boat, an

Englishman. One day, we left the harbour under motor power and got out into the broad lake. The wind was blowing, we set our sails, and then we cut the motor. All we could hear was the blowing of the wind in the sails and we were underway. And the guy looked at me and he looked at his watch and he said, 'Well, it's nine o'clock. There are guys that are getting into their offices right now who are going to work for twenty-five years so they can do what I'm doing right now.' He didn't start off to be a sailor, but he was doing what he wanted to do."

This leads to two questions: why does it take so long for people to identify their passions? And why do they often not follow their passions, especially in their career choices? The first answer is about awareness and insight: knowing yourself and being clear about your passions. The second answer is about circumstances and courage. Following your passion into a career often involves risk taking and sacrifice. It's not always easy, but it can be very rewarding.

> "I forgot that having fun is an option."
> —Michael Held, CEO and Co-founder, LifeSpeak Inc.

CHUCK'S STORY

Chuck was a wonderful high school teacher who had the respect and affection of legions of his students. He told me how he ended up as an educator. He'd been working in advertising, writing commercials and ad copy. Given how bright and funny he was, it was no surprise that he was successful at it. But he wasn't feeling fulfilled.

One day, he came home at about 10:30 in the morning. Surprised to see him, his wife asked if he was OK.

"Is there something wrong?"

"I can't do it anymore."

"Do what?"

"Write this stuff for these clients."

"What are you talking about?"

"I'm going to resign."

"*What*? What are you going to do instead?"

"I've been thinking of going to teachers' college and becoming a high school teacher."

"Chuck, we've got three children. What are we going to live on?"

"We'll work it out. I just can't face another twenty years of this."

Chuck went back to school for a year while working part-time. It was intense, but he got his certificate and became an inspiring and entertaining teacher. He was in the right groove, doing what he truly wanted and loved to do. He was living his passion, living in sync with himself, and doing work that was congruent with his authentic self. As a result, he was fulfilled and his students loved him. It was the right fit.

CHAPTER 27

THE PATH BEHIND YOU AND THE ROAD AHEAD

We all make choices throughout our lives. Where you live, where you work, whom you live with—these are often results of choices you made along the way. How did you come to be a carpenter in Calgary or an artist in Santa Fe? If you own a bookstore in Halifax or work in a hospital in Atlanta, what led you there? Some decisions were made quickly; others took time. Some resulted from economic necessity, others because an opportunity suddenly appeared and seemed appealing at the time. Some seemed obvious; others you agonized over. And in some cases you just went with the flow or drifted into things without a lot of thought.

In reflecting on the odyssey that brought me to be a stress specialist in Oakville, Ontario, I identified a number of pivotal decisions and forks in the road where I chose one path over another. Here they are on a diagram, beginning with my high school graduation.

A Lifetime of Choices

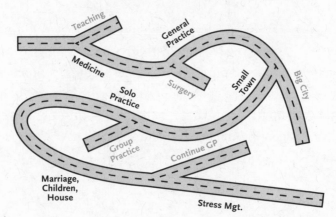

The initial decision was to go into medicine instead of teaching. Then I chose to leave Toronto to do my internship in Edmonton, Alberta. After that intense year, I had to decide on a specialty. Surgery appealed to me, but first I wanted to get some experience and to have some adventures before starting a residency. I tried to get into the trauma hospital in Birmingham, England, but my visa was held up so I went to work in the Canadian Arctic. Within six memorable months in Inuvik, Northwest Territories, it became clear that I enjoyed general practice, with its variety and focus on patient interaction. After my year in the Arctic, and a second year doing general practice and emergency work in Jerusalem, I came back to Canada and made another decision. Toronto had become too big for my liking so I moved to a small town of 50,000 people with a wonderful hospital. I've been in Oakville ever since.

I started in a group practice but after a year decided to set up my own solo practice, a huge investment and commitment. Twelve years later I got married, we bought a house, and we had two children—big and happy decisions, all of them. On the work front, I started to learn about stress theory and stress counselling in 1981 and was immediately hooked. I found the whole field fascinating and started to incorporate it into my family practice. Then I started to see patients on referral from other doctors. By 1984, it was clear that this was what I wanted to do full-time— and it was competing for time with my general practice duties. (As a friend of mine put it, "You've been riding two horses for four years. It's time to choose one and get off the other.") So, in 1985, I gave up family medicine to devote my time exclusively to stress management and lifestyle counselling. I have never looked back or had a minute of regret. Around the same time, I added public speaking to the mix. Since then, I've slowly evolved to lecturing more and seeing fewer patients. Another big decision came in 1989: to write a book. Then to write a second and a third and a fourth and now this, my fifth.

In the diagram "A Lifetime of Choices," I highlighted the five major decisions as forks in the road where I specifically chose one path over another. There were, as recounted above, many other choices along the way as well.

Your Lifetime Journey

On the diagram below, think about *your* voyage from the time you left high school and started to make your own important choices. Think of the significant moments, the decisions you made — particularly about your work — and what path you *didn't* take if it involved choosing one direction over another. This exercise has two purposes. One is to reflect back on the trajectory of your life so far. The other is to help you realize that you can continue to make choices, to opt for new directions if what you're doing has been dissatisfying or has become stale.

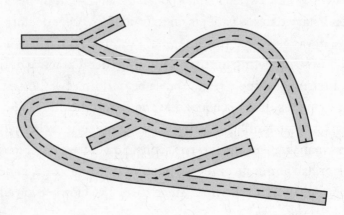

The Learning Curve

This leads to another issue. What you're doing now might have been just dandy when you started but might no longer hold much appeal for you. This might make sense if you look at the shape of a learning curve.

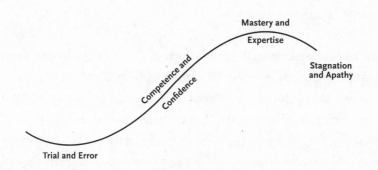

Every time we learn a new skill we go through a stage of trial and error where we get used to the new routine. If you want to see this in action, watch little kids as they try to master their new bicycle without the training wheels. Hang around the bunny hill where novices are learning to ski. Sit in on a beginner music class and listen to the squeaks made by rookie reed players trying to play notes on a clarinet. Think of learning to use a computer, serve a tennis ball, or drive a car.

After a while you catch on and get pretty good at the new activity. And as your competence increases, so does your confidence. Pretty soon you're doing the new skill with ease. You've developed a level of mastery such that you can drive while listening to the radio, play the piano without looking at the keys, and so on. Then something interesting happens. You reach a plateau where the activity isn't as interesting anymore. It's lost its novelty or challenge and may even become boring. This is the stage of stagnation and apathy. At this point, you might look for new challenges: tougher ski runs, more difficult piano music, etc.

Now let's apply this to a job. As with any acquired skill, your work can become rote and routine. You don't get the same buzz anymore. That's when you might start looking for a change. We all need new challenges to keep life interesting and stimulating and to keep our edges honed.

When I first saw this curve, I noted that I had made changes in my work life roughly every four to five years without even realizing the pattern. For example, in 1981, I got interested in stress management and stopped delivering babies. In 1985, I gave up my family practice to do stress counselling full-time. In 1989, I started writing my first book. In 1994, the book came out and I started doing a lot more public speaking. In 1997, I began my second book. In 2000, I started writing a weekly column on the Internet (for the Canadian web site canoe.ca). In 2003, my third book came out. All the while, I was creating new speeches and seminars and learning new information to share with my patients and audiences. It's been an ongoing process of renewal, a professional evolution that has kept my work fresh and fun. And it has continually moved me closer to my original love—teaching.

Cindy's Story: Sequential Passions and Changing Midstream

In 2010, I heard a radio interview with Cindy Krysak, a physics professor who had resigned her university position to become an apprentice electrician. I called her immediately and asked if

I could talk to her about this dramatic occupational shift. Here is her story.

"I started doing mechanical things at an early age. I took apart a bicycle and then put it back together again, probably around six or seven years old. I still remember the focus. It was fascinating. My parents bought me this set of gears that sit on a peg board. The gears all fit together, and then you can make the gears all work and turn, and the little elastics go around. I loved that; I absolutely hungered for that.

"My mom recognized this and gave me a set of tools for Christmas. I was thirteen or fourteen. My parents encouraged me through everything. Their philosophy was enrichment. They were wonderful that way. My father was a mining engineer and my mom was an artist and a writer.

"At age eleven I decided that I wanted to be a physicist. My father was interested in science and he had me read *Scientific American* articles to him. He was going blind so I read aloud. Physics is an examination of reality. You can logically go about examining it, testing it, and confirming what reality is. I wanted to be an experimentalist. I've always liked mechanical things. I always wanted to do the practical. I like problem solving with mechanical aspects. I like the creation of experiments, asking questions, and testing them. It was more like that is who I was. It's like it was a passion about being me. I was a physicist.

"I loved being a physicist. I really enjoyed it. It was absolutely the right thing for me at the time. It was perfect for me for a long, long time. I was there many years and then only at the very end did I become less enthused. I wasn't getting as much emotional feedback from the work. I was changing. I wasn't flourishing.

"Finally, there was a turning point. I asked myself, *OK, now what are you going to do? It's an opportunity to rethink. Am I bound by the choices I made when I was eleven?* And then I took a sabbatical year off to be at home with my kids doing art and writing a couple of small educational books on physics. During that time the idea that I would not go back became evident. But what was I going to do instead?

"I got a fixer-upper and was rewiring the house. I was having fun. It was soothing; it was relaxing, enjoyable. It was thoughtfulness, problem solving; it was physical and a lot of mechanical motions, building things, and constructing things. I was an experimental physicist so I spent a lot of time in the lab creating things. That part was the best.

"So, then, they happened to have an intake for electrical apprentices at the joint apprenticeship council. And when I got there it was like meeting a whole lot of guys who were just like me. I loved mechanical problem solving and it has just been very enjoyable ever since.

"Every day you're using your tools and mucking about, confronting reality. In physics you could do a research project and have some very fancy ideas. But here it is, 'Well, we have to get the electrical service from here to the roof.' It's a different mindset completely. So the problem-solving attitude is totally different and I love that. I love that whole 'there is no unsolvable problem' attitude in the electrical trade, so you're in there making it happen, whatever the problem is. And I like that. That's fun.

"The electrical trade may not have been the best thing for me earlier on because part of me really needed to follow the earlier passion of being a physicist and exercising that kind of problem solving with my mind, which I needed to do. In the electrical trade, the focus has shifted for me. It's less stressful because I can rely on my skills that I can learn and practice. I don't have to rely on 'Oh, I hope that this solution I've created is the right solution according to my peers.' No! Does the light turn on? You're done. It's great! Move on to the next problem.

"So, here I am working in a trade that I feel is challenging, rewarding, and exciting. It requires me to be logical, it requires a great deal of mechanical aptitude skill. It's the honesty of the work that I love the most. It is the honesty of the fellows I work with. We're here to get a job done and we get the job done. I love that! I absolutely love the whole cleanliness to that.

"And for myself, I enjoy learning and developing that part of my brain, which is similar but different than that part of my brain that I had to develop in order to succeed in physics."

Passions and careers can change over a lifetime if we're open to that possibility. Artist Grandma Moses didn't start painting seriously until she was in her late seventies. Wherever you are on your life's journey, stop and take stock of where you are and whether you feel happy and fulfilled. Keep exploring possible new avenues to pursue. You're never too old to keep growing and changing.

CHAPTER 28

DEALING WITH OBSTACLES —
AND REALITY!

Following your passion to find work you love is the ideal. For many people — perhaps most — this is a pipe dream. It may not be achievable. A friend of mine said, "That concept sounds pretty elitist to me. Most people have to go out and just get a job." Another said, "Isn't that a pretty hedonistic argument? If everybody did that, who would be the garbage collectors?" All these comments are true and valid. Many individuals may not have the education required to follow their dream. Or they may not have the money to pursue the necessary education. Or there may be no work available in the field that fuels their passion. Or they may not have the talent required to succeed. What then?

There are several ways to answer that question. First and foremost is education. And there are many ways to do that:

- **Formal education**
  Finish high school and then decide what extra education you'll need to get into the field you want. It might be university; it might be a community college for specific skills training. Internet courses and even degree programs are offered online.

- **Part-time or informal education**
  Legions of folks go to night school or take weekend courses while working full-time during the day. It takes longer,

but they end up with the education or training they need. That's how I schooled myself in stress theory and stress management while still a full-time family physician. I read extensively, went to seminars, and learned from mentors, all on evenings and weekends. My wife later told me that she thought I was a workaholic at the beginning of our relationship. What fuelled me over those four years was my passion for what I was learning in my off hours. I couldn't wait to get at it in the evenings I set aside for study. That was both the incentive to spend the time and energy but also the clue that I was on the right track.

- **On-the-job training leading to credentialing**
  For example, there is an option at some universities for accounting students to do co-op work that counts toward their CPA designation.

- **Apprenticeship**
  One of my patients wanted to become a cabinetmaker. She was eighteen and really excited about it. She found a skilled artisan and became his apprentice. She learned from the ground up, gaining experience and learning from a master.

A second approach is experience.

- **Work experience**
  You might start and learn from entry-level jobs in factories, banks, offices, and small start-up companies that need administrative or assistant positions filled. Many people start out in the book business by working with an agent or publisher, doing a lot of mundane tasks while learning the ropes.

Bars, taverns, restaurants, and resorts hire and train staff in bartending, hostessing, or managing.

- **Volunteer work and internships**
  Another way to get experience is through volunteer work in the area that excites you. Internships are available in many fields. Ask if you can help a nonprofit group on one of their projects.

- **Networking**
  Do anything you can to meet people who are doing the kind of work you want to do. Build a network of role models who inspire you and mentors who might help you pursue your passion. Dr. Matthew Budd at Harvard was invaluable to me in this regard, taking me under his wing, introducing me to his colleagues in the stress field, recommending books and courses for me to take, and directing my learning for several years.

- **Travel**
  An often-overlooked way to gain experience is through travel. Lots of high school grads go backpacking in another country or continent. You can do it on the cheap, taking jobs along the way, learning about people, different cultures, and the world in general. It might be an opportunity to learn specific skills and other languages, and to get general experience in being on your own and learning self-reliance. You can build a network of relationships. (You might even fall in love and never come home—but don't tell your parents I said that!) Perhaps most important, you can learn a lot about yourself, which will serve you well in eventually choosing your career path. More awareness leads to better choices.

What about Money? Overcoming Financial Obstacles

Finding the money to pursue the education and career you feel passionate about is a real and common problem. But there are ways to deal with that too:

- Apply for scholarships if you're a good student.

- Look into service clubs such as Rotary that help fund worthy students to continue their education.

- Check out bursaries available for students in need.

- Consider student loans, another option.

- Trade education funding for service. Several students in my class had their schooling paid for by the Canadian military in exchange for a set number of years as army doctors after they graduated.

- Find paid educational opportunities such as apprenticeships.

- Look into programs with a paid co-op every other semester, so that you have an income every four months.

- Work part-time while you pursue further education or wait for your big break, to reduce your debt load and/or help cover expenses. Many aspiring actors, musicians, writers, and artists have worked in restaurants or pubs, in construction, or done weekend shifts in retail.

- Briefly adjust your lifestyle—go on a budget for a couple of years. Move into less expensive housing while you're in school or retraining.

- Save aggressively while you stick it out with your present employer, until you can finish training in another field or find the job you really want. It will help to have a goal or "finish line" to aim for.

- Finally, if you live in an economically depressed area where only menial jobs exist, perhaps consider an even larger decision—to move to another town or part of the country where job opportunities are more plentiful.

If you read biographies of successful people, you find that most of them struggled, sacrificed, and suffered setbacks. Success is almost never a straight line upward. As the old clichés go, "there's no free lunch" and "there are no shortcuts in life." You have to pay your dues in any field of endeavour. And there's nothing wrong with a little hard work. Or even a *lot* of hard work. It has integrity to it.

> "To reach any significant goal, you must leave your comfort zone."
> — Hyrum W. Smith

Graham's Story: Lifelong Passion Meets Workplace Reality

Graham Kitching started young. Like really young—age five. He was a car guy from the get-go. His parents bought him his first model car, a 1955 black Chevy Corvette, which he assembled with his dad. He added other toy cars and a roll-out mat, and sat for hours "driving" them. At age six, he started watching TV shows about cars. *The Dukes of Hazzard* was a big hit. Watching how they worked on the cars and drove them around got his adrenalin pumping every episode.

By eleven, Graham was watching TV shows that showed how to do brake jobs, how to do engines. He was fascinated and inspired to learn what makes a car go. He loved the mechanics behind it.

In his first year of high school, Graham got right into machine shop. By then he was very tech oriented and loved working with his hands. In grade eleven, he signed up for automotive shop. He learned how to take things apart and put them back together. "That's how everything fell together. My old passion of building model cars and watching TV shows and now I'm putting it to use and saying, 'OK, this is what I want to do.'"

Graham's grade twelve teacher saw his talent and passion and encouraged him to do a major project in his final year: to take a car apart and assemble it again, all on his own. He went in at lunchtime and after school to work on it. And he found it thrilling.

That same year, with the help of his parents, he bought his first car, an '87 Mustang. He was sixteen. "I've learned a lot about cars not only from mentors and teachers but by doing it myself; saying, 'The heck with it. I'll figure it out myself.'"

After high school, Graham went to a community college, taking a one-year apprenticeship program. It was an entry-level automotive-industry course teaching electronics, computers, and different mechanical and fuel systems. He loved it. "Every second... bring it on. No matter what the obstacle was, even if the homework was challenging, I didn't care. I just said, 'It's fine. I love this field. I want to be in it. I don't want anything else.' I knew I loved working with my hands, getting dirty. It's part of my life. It's in my blood."

Graham finished his first year of college and, then, something unexpected happened. "I hit a roadblock in my career path. I worked in a couple of auto shops and it became very tedious.

Days were long, people were demanding, it became unenjoyable. Kind of like the flame burnt out a little. It was the customers. They'd demand, 'I want this and I want it for cheap.' When you're working in the field, you don't have time to learn and look and really enjoy what you're doing. It's just, 'Get the car in, take it apart, get it out the door. As long as we're making money off of it, nobody cares.' So now I've got to do this really fast and I've got the boss breathing down my neck. It just didn't seem to fit. It didn't seem to suit who I was and what I did.

"So that's when I said, 'This isn't fun anymore. I want to enjoy this.' That's when I realized I enjoyed this as a hobby, doing it on my own time, at home at my own pace, on my own car."

Graham needed something to excite him again. He wanted to stay in the mechanical world and found that his community college offered a three-year mechanical engineering program dealing with automotive design. "I said right away, 'That's it. That's what I want to do.' It was taking the automotive mechanics to the next level, getting to the science behind the vehicle and how they're designed and manufactured. The light came back, the fire came back, and I said, 'That's what I need to get into.'"

First year was generic: basic engineering, mathematical problems, different computer systems. In second year, "they hit you—BAM—right in the face: automotive programs coming from everywhere. It was perfect. Second and third year were great. I kept my marks up and it was still very enjoyable. After college, I said, 'That's it. I want to be in this field.'"

Oddly enough, his first job opportunity after graduation wasn't in the automotive field. It was still related to mechanical engineering, so he decided to give it a shot. The company did custom engineering in steel fabrications and his boss was a very good coach. "He got me settled into this engineering world. I struggled with it at first, but after a few months, I said, 'This feels good. This is something different, but I still like it. I love the automotive stuff, but I like it more as a hobby. It still burns inside me. But I like the mechanical engineering side of steel fabrications, welding, getting your hands dirty, but it's a different scope than automotive.'"

After nine months, the work got slow so Graham had to take some time off. He sent out resumés to engineering departments while working on his car. He landed a job in a heating, ventilation, and air-conditioning company, and found it a perfect fit.

"It's the total opposite end, but it's still in the mechanical world. I used to work in automotive, but now I'm into heating, ventilation, and sheet metal. It's funny because all my life I figured, *I want to be a car guy*. But I think that, the whole time I was saying that, I didn't necessarily mean I wanted to *work* in the car field. I wanted that passion just to be in my life, whether as a hobby or helping friends out or things like that. So it was still part of my life and I think that's what made me content. I have the mechanical engineering side that I wanted, but I still have my hobby, which is automotive. To me, it all balances out in a perfect world."

Common Themes

Throughout this section on passions and career choice, I've cited a number of different stories. But they all have a few similar themes, common threads that flow through them:

1. **Each person went through a process to find their way to what they're happy doing now.**

They started with an idea, set a goal, pursued a path to reach it, made adjustments, overcame obstacles, got help from others, and eventually found their niche.

2. **They enjoyed the journey as well as the outcome.**

   Kris Kristofferson said, "I was in heaven even though I wasn't making any money as a writer." Shelley Posen reflected: "I knew I made the right choice whenever I was doing fieldwork, whenever I was in a fisherman's house or on the ice of Lake Champlain talking to guys about what they were doing. I would think to myself, *Here I am in this Newfoundland fisherman's house listening to him talking while his kids mill around and his wife bakes bread — how fabulous is that?*"

3. **They all had considerable support from significant people, most especially their parents.**

   ROB: "I should give credit to my parents and everybody. Not once did anyone ever try to lead me down any sort of path they wanted for me. I had the full support of absolutely everybody when it became clear what it was I wanted to do."

   GRAHAM: "Throughout the whole process my parents were very supportive of me. They helped me with paying for college, and they supported me in any way possible. When you have people behind you 100 percent, it's very uplifting."

   CINDY: "My parents encouraged me for everything. Their philosophy was enrichment. They were wonderful that way."

4. **Money never came up in any of the discussions or stories I've shared—nor did it even come up as a consideration.**
   If anything, most people sacrificed financially to follow their dream, and many acknowledged that they would never get rich in the careers they were pursuing. Here's how Cindy put it: "There are trade-offs and sacrifices. As a graduate student in physics, you don't make a lot of money and you spend a lot of years studying and it's a sacrifice. I like money but not enough to sacrifice my whole life for it."

5. **They all followed their passions with zest and determination.**
   Even as they encountered obstacles or as their passions sometimes shifted or took different directions, they continued to follow what Joseph Campbell calls their "bliss."

There are countless stories of people who found their careers in various ways. In many cases they followed their passions early; in many *more*, they found their way to their careers by trial and error, experimentation, and experience. Find people whose life paths can be instructive to you. Then listen to their stories and see if they can help to guide, direct, and inspire you.

CHAPTER 29

OTHER VIEWS AND FINAL THOUGHTS

I've been collecting articles and anecdotes for years on the subject of passions and career choice. But I also like to read material that conflicts with or even contradicts my own thinking. I like to challenge my premises to see if they actually hold up. This muddies the water a bit. After all, issues are simple when they're only black or white. But in life it's rarely that clear. Most things are in the grey zone. And it's important to acknowledge that fact and explore other sides of the issue.

In 2015, Ryan Holmes wrote an article for Entrepreneur.com titled "When You Shouldn't Follow Your Heart." In it he suggests allowing your "calling" to come to you. Most people don't have a clear sense of their passions from the get-go. Only by having a variety of experiences do things become clear. Holmes says, "Over the years, real passions grow clearer and mere distractions fade away. At the same time, critical skills have time to develop." He went on to develop a tech tool that became a highly successful company called Hootsuite.

Similarly, Cal Newport argued in a *New York Times* article that "follow your passion" makes sense for people who are clear about their passion but that "this philosophy puts a lot of pressure on the rest of us. . . . We may end up missing our true calling" or experiencing self-doubt that can "generate anxiety and chronic job-hopping." He then offers a simple premise: "The traits that lead people to love their work are general and have little to do with a job's specifics." Faced with three very appealing career paths in his senior year of college, Newport was "confident that all three of my career options could be transformed into a source of passion.... I knew that my sense of fulfillment would grow over time as I became better at my job. So I worked hard and, as my competence grew, so did my engagement." He ends with a piece of advice: "Passion is not something you follow. It's something that will follow you as you put in the hard work to become valuable to the world."

So how do we reconcile these different but valid points of view? First, by acknowledging that passions are not always clear and often don't develop early. Then by considering the following thoughts and suggestions:

- **Follow your passion if and when you can.**
  Keep your eyes and ears open for opportunities.

- **Be open to new experiences and see what happens.**
  Look for opportunities to try new things. Be willing to leave your comfort zone.

- **Travel, experiment, seek out adventures and activities to widen your horizons and introduce you to possibilities you might not have considered.**
  I went to the Canadian Arctic for adventure and experience — and that's where I learned how much I enjoyed general practice medicine.

- **Take note of the things that interest you, that you gravitate toward, and that you avoid or dislike.**
  And especially pay attention to the things that really excite you.

- **Talk to people who are doing things you'd like to be doing.**
Ask them how they did it. Seek out their guidance and
wisdom.

- **Read biographies and autobiographies for inspiration and
encouragement—and for a reality check that any road you
choose will have bumps and curves.**
Most lives don't unfold neatly, cleanly, and in a linear fashion.
They're complicated and convoluted. Successful people don't
usually rocket straight to the top without setbacks, obstacles,
and even failures. That's what makes biographies and autobiographies so fascinating.

    One particular book I love is about a guy who went to
work as a bank clerk. He was doing well when his father's
farm started to fail. So he left a promising career to return
home, working on the farm for ten years to help his dad keep
things going. When war broke out, he tried to enlist but got
rejected because he failed the vision test. Undaunted, he
went back after memorizing the eye chart, was accepted, and
served overseas, rising to the rank of captain. After the war,
he went into a men's clothing store business. The venture
failed so he got a job in local government. Eventually he
drifted into civic politics, where he showed great promise.
People liked and trusted him so he moved up the ranks, first
locally, then in his state, and finally nationally, where he was
a senator for ten years. Only upon the death of the sitting
president did Vice President Harry S. Truman become the
thirty-third president of the United States. But the trajectory
of his career was anything but straight and smooth.

- **Network with others to find openings.**
  Let people know what you're interested in. That's how I found my way to Oakville, Ontario, in 1971. A friend and colleague knew I was coming back to Canada and would be looking for a job. He told me about an opening I would never have known about otherwise.

- **If, like most people, you can't hit the career bull's-eye on the first try, keep evolving to get closer to what pleases you most.**
  Don't be afraid to apply for new jobs or even to change companies in pursuit of a better fit.

- **Accept that setbacks, detours, wrong turns, closed doors, dead ends, and even failure will be part of the process in pursuing your goals and dreams.**
  British business writer Charles Handy said, "Getting it wrong is part of getting it right."

- **Be determined and persistent.**
  Don't give up.

- **Be willing to work hard.**
  Nothing worthwhile in life ever comes easily. Everyone has to "pay their dues."

- **Be prepared for a journey and be patient with the process.**
  Flip Wilson was a popular comedian who had his own TV show from 1970 to 74, winning a Golden Globe and two Emmys. When he appeared to "burst onto the scene," he was called an overnight sensation. "Yeah," he said, "it only took twenty-five years."

- **Have the courage of your convictions.**

  Dare to walk a different path from what others are doing or expect you to do. For example, women were a rare breed in fields like mathematics and engineering until recent generations. A woman I know ran a program for women in nontraditional trades such as plumbing and welding. Many men had to do some courageous trailblazing when they decided to become ballet dancers.

  > It's a given that to succeed in any line of work, you're going to have to work hard. It might as well be at something you enjoy.

- **Be prepared to make changes within your chosen field until you find the right fit for you.**

  When I was in med school, there was a saying that "there are a thousand jobs in Medicine." Everything from surgery to psychiatry, research to sports medicine, being a teacher to being a coroner. The same can be said for most fields of endeavour.

- **Even if your overall job doesn't feel like your "sweet spot," find things within your job that you really love and enjoy.**

  As a family doctor, my three favourite things were interacting with children, counselling, and suturing lacerations. One woman was a lawyer in a nonprofit organization, but what really lit her up was designing posters for their various public events.

- **Design or create aspects of your work that you can feel passionate about.**

  Look for ways to make your job more enjoyable and meaningful. In his excellent TED book, *Why We Work*, author

Barry Schwartz discusses a series of interviews conducted by researcher Amy Wrzesniewski. She cited several examples of hospital custodians who went beyond their job descriptions in small ways to show care and consideration for patients and their families. Their jobs might have been routine or even mundane, but they went out of their way to do small things for patients that weren't in their formal job descriptions. Wrzesniewski calls this "job crafting," and it changed the whole tone and attitude that these custodians brought to their work every day. It gave meaning, purpose, and pride to their jobs. They were there to help patients, not just clean the floors.

- **Start a new initiative at work that can ignite your passion.**
  Ask for permission to design and pursue a project in line with the company's focus but not currently part of its program. It might be developing a new product, researching a related and exciting area of interest, or starting a mentorship program.

- **Develop relationships with people at work that can be a source of pleasure.**
  Sometimes the work itself won't delight you, but the people you meet fill the pleasure gap. If you work with a group or team you really enjoy, it can make a big difference in how you feel about going to work every day.

- **Indulge your passion away from work.**
  This is what Graham did to keep his love of cars in his life. Find other outlets for your passion even if you can't find it in your work. I knew a physician who liked his job but didn't love it. He was an excellent doctor and took his work

seriously. But he was fuelled most by his passion for sailing in the summer and skiing in the winter. That's where he felt most alive, exhilarated, and at peace. Community concert bands, orchestras, choirs, theatre groups, book clubs, art classes, folk dancing, sports leagues, tennis and golf clubs, curling rinks, rock bands, jazz ensembles, quilting groups — all of these are filled with people who haven't given up their day jobs but come alive in the evenings or weekends when they can "do their thing."

> The word "amateur" comes from the Latin verb "*amare*," which means "to love." You don't have to be a professional to love your recreational activities and pursue your passions.

- **If you can't find work that you're passionate about, consider starting your own venture.**
  Forge your own new path. This is how a lot of start-ups begin.

- **Finally, accept that you may not find work that matches your passion.**
  But whatever job you do, do it to the best of your ability. It might even lead you to feel passionate about it.

A Final Thought

I asked Cindy if there were any lessons she'd learned or wisdom that her experiences have taught her.

"Well, really the only essential thing is that if you know yourself and

> Where availability ends, creativity and innovation begin.

understand yourself, and start exploring who you are, and become aware and awake to your own behaviours and thought patterns, the easier it will be to choose an occupation. It's a self-awareness that is a crucial element not just for career choices but for all your life."

CONCLUSION

MUSIC AS METAPHOR

CONCLUSION

MUSIC AS METAPHOR

In ninth grade I blew into a trombone for the first time. The note was F. I've been playing off and on ever since. Music is an enriching part of my life. But I only have a range of two and a half octaves. Glenn Miller and Tommy Dorsey could play *four*—I should be so talented! In bands and orchestras, trumpets play high notes, trombones play low notes—and tubas play *really* low notes. The trombone isn't designed to play clarinet music, nor can flutes play bassoon parts. Every instrument has a range. Once musicians figure out where they fit, where their strengths are, making music becomes easier, more satisfying—and more enjoyable. The concept of range applies to life in general—especially living within the bounds of our own physiology and aptitudes.

Tempo is another aspect of music that performers have to consider. As with all amateur orchestras, our Oakville Wind Orchestra has to decide how fast to play the pieces we perform. Professionals can play at dizzying speeds—I can't even *read* the notes as fast as top musicians can play them! Our conductor has to find a speed that is close to the composer's intention but still manageable for us to keep up with. Too slow and it sounds like a dirge. Too fast and we stumble all over the notes. The analogy to the pace at which we choose to live our lives is obvious.

And then there's rhythm. Our orchestra plays everything from classical music to jazz, Broadway tunes to rock, overtures to marches. Some pieces are fast, some slow; some in strict time, some in syncopated time or swing. The best concerts contain a variety of these elements, just as a balanced life should.

In life, we function best when we find rhythms that suit us and feel comfortable, while also being open to some variety and flexibility.

As my musically talented son Jaime pointed out to me, music also includes pauses and rests. These are places where some instruments stop playing while others pick up the melody — or when the whole ensemble goes quiet for dramatic effect. In our own lives, it's vitally important that we also stop and pause — not for *dramatic* effect, but to reduce our stress, restore our energy, and enhance our enjoyment of life.

Harmony is another major aspect of ensemble music. Whether it's the lush, sweeping music of Tchaikovsky or the fabulous blend of the Beatles, making beautiful music isn't just about how well you play or sing *your* part, but how well you mesh with others. It's about listening, balancing, co-operating, and blending. In life, it's helpful to know ourselves so that we can design lives that are aligned with who we are. But it's also important to understand one another in order to live and work in harmony with *them*.

This also ties in with values. In ensemble music, it's important that players leave their egos at the door and do whatever it takes to serve the music and the needs of the group as a whole. Sometimes this means letting other people have the solos while you take a less prominent part. We're taught that when your section doesn't have the melody (often the case for trombones), you should play softer so you don't drown out the main tune. Our conductor calls this "being wallpaper while the main colours shine through."

> Life is a lot easier when you get along with other people.

One more thing: when you *love* the music you're playing, it fuels your *passion*. When you don't, it dulls it. Like legions of kids, I was signed up for piano lessons at age six. My teacher chose the pieces I was to learn along with the thrill of practising scales. I was an indifferent student, although I liked *some* of the pieces. But when I was twelve, we found a new teacher, Harvey Silver, who taught me to play the sheet music of current popular songs. And *I* got to pick the songs. My interest exploded into enthusiasm and I started playing for fun. It was a completely different experience. Practising was no longer a chore. Sometimes I'd even sing along with some of the music (often with my twin sister at my side, singing Broadway show tunes). I still have all those books and sheet music, which I can still play enjoyably.

When I think of living an authentic life and living in harmony with yourself, I picture a "sweet spot" of comfort and balance, but it's not necessarily restrictive. There is a circle outside the circle, so to speak, where we can range freely when we choose to do so.

I'm not advocating a life where we only seek ease and complacency. I'm all for working hard to achieve goals and to even push against our physiological limits at times. There are occasions when we must leave our comfort zones: out of necessity, to accept challenges, to make progress, to fit into new situations, to get along with others, or for the variety and adventure that life can offer. But we should do so at times of our own choosing, to the extent that we can handle it, and with the knowledge that there may be discomfort and stress involved. It's OK to be less congruent—or to stretch the bounds of what is possible for us. We just need to know what we're in for and to be prepared for what we may be up against and what the cost might be. Here again, more awareness can lead to better choices — and better *calculated* choices.

In this book, I have discussed elements of physiology (time, speed, sleep), psychology (personality traits), and philosophy (values and passions). My focus embraces physical, mental, emotional, and spiritual health, all of which are important to consider when designing authentic lives that are aligned with who we are as individuals.

Let me make an important distinction here. In an age of selfies and self-promotion on social media, the concept of being true to yourself might be misconstrued. Self-awareness is not the same as self-absorption or self-indulgence, or even outright selfishness — none of which I endorse. When I talk about self-awareness, it is in the context of self-honesty, self-care, and self-respect, thus allowing you to make better choices and to be kind to yourself.

> "It is never too late to be what you might have been."
> —George Eliot

There are three main messages I want to convey:

1. Get to know yourself better so you can make better choices in your life. Live authentically as much as you can.

2. Step out of your comfort zone. Choose not to be limited by your biology, genetics, or the social or economic circumstances you were born into. But be aware of — and prepared for — the challenges you will face in doing so.

3. Live and let live. Live in a way that's true to *yourself* and let *others* do the same. Don't try to push, cajole, or coerce

them into being something or someone they're not. Listen to other people's preferences instead of dictating your own. This is especially important advice for parents and teachers — especially if they're acting to further their own interest, live vicariously, or to fulfill their own ambitions.

Changing a lifetime of attitudes and behaviours may seem daunting at first. Our identities and habits have been built over a long period of time, and are the result of many external influences. But living in conflict with your inner self is actually more difficult — and more unpleasant — than finding and befriending the person you really are. As a doctor and educator, and from personal experience, I can tell you categorically that living in harmony with your true self leads to a joy and comfort you'll wish you'd found much earlier in life.

When people struggle to be what they're not designed or inclined to be, the result is high stress, inner conflict, poor health, and general unhappiness. If we live in ways that are authentic and true to ourselves, we can lead more fulfilling, productive, and happy lives. I hope this book will help you find that kind of harmony in your own life.

I leave you now with a call to action. Ask yourself, What's one step I can take, one thing I can do right now to begin reclaiming my authentic self? And then get started!

ACKNOWLEDGEMENTS

This book began with a book—two books, really: Jeremy Rifkin's *Time Wars* and *What You Can Change and What You Can't* by Martin Seligman. They motivated me to explore the many ways we live out of sync with our own natures and preferences. My first acknowledgement goes to Jeremy and Martin for planting the seed for this book.

I started a file back in 1995 called "Round Pegs in Square Holes," thinking it might be a good idea for a follow-up to my first book, *Always Change a Losing Game*. I kept adding notes and articles to that file over the years, writing three other books in the meantime. But I never gave up on fully developing the idea of reducing stress by living in harmony with oneself. This twenty-three-year odyssey was aided immeasurably by the encouragement, support, and generous gift of time from many people. I want to acknowledge and thank each of them by name.

The late Clare McKeon, my editor at Key Porter Books, was the first person to validate my idea and encourage me to pursue it. She also reviewed early drafts of two sections before her tragic and untimely passing. This book is dedicated to her.

My wife, Susan McArthur, was the second person to express enthusiasm for both the idea and the working title. She's been consistently supportive ever since, as she's been with all my books. She also read the manuscript, giving me her usual sensitive and insightful feedback.

Dr. Brian Little has been a wonderfully kind and generous mentor in the field of personality science and specifically introversion and extraversion. Aside from all he has taught me, Brian carefully reviewed and critiqued the entire section on introverts and extraverts.

Judy Knapp, my former office nurse, continues to patiently read everything I write and give me important feedback and ongoing encouragement. Her years of support and friendship mean a lot to me.

Dr. Robbie Campbell, friend and colleague since we interned together in Edmonton, has been an enthusiastic cheerleader for all of my books, and was again the first to return the manuscript with his comments and useful input.

Drs. Alan Brown and Karl O'Sullivan are esteemed psychiatric colleagues whose wisdom and expertise over the years have been invaluable in my work with patients. They both carefully read the manuscript and provided detailed comments and suggestions, most of which I acted on.

Dr. Steve Swallow, my psychology colleague who reviewed the manuscript, gave me insightful feedback, and has been an unfailingly cheerful source of support for my writing.

Dr. Peter Norlin, a lifelong friend and source of much wisdom, critiqued the manuscript with care and kindness, paying special attention to tone as well as content.

Dr. Terry Riley, esteemed colleague and friend, and Joanne Riley, voracious reader, reviewed the manuscript and gave it the thumbs up along with helpful comments and input.

Mark Jesty, from the Institute for Management Studies (IMS), lent me his keen ear for nuance and impact. His astute advice and monumental support over the years have opened many doors for me.

Katie Davidman, my niece and experienced therapist, gave me valuable insight into several issues, caught me out on a few details, and shared her knowledge of recent research in extremely helpful ways.

Dr. Colin Shapiro, sleep expert at the University of Toronto, kindly agreed to review my sleep chapters and then generously came to my office to share his suggestions and corrections, and to give me a three-hour tutorial, complete with copies of several of his own books.

Susan Cain, whose bestselling book *Quiet* was a very valuable resource for me, reviewed parts of my introversion chapters, sent a note of encouragement, and gave me permission to cite some of her information.

My interview subjects Rob (not his real name), Shelley Posen, Cindy Krysak, and Graham Kitching, and my breakfast table panel of Bob, Paul, and Sheryl took considerable time out of their busy lives and showed great interest in sharing their personal stories with me.

My son, Andrew Posen, carefully reviewed the manuscript, gave me detailed and sensitive feedback, and showed a level of wisdom that has always impressed me.

My twin sister, Karen Davidman, enthusiastically read the manuscript, provided helpful comments, and gave me huge amounts of encouragement and support—as she has done throughout my life.

Karolina Luburic, my amazing assistant, who deciphered my rough notes (often scrawled at night in the dark) and typed up multiple drafts, was my invaluable tech guru and brightened every day she spent in my office.

Beverley Slopen, my heaven-sent literary agent, has guided, advised, encouraged, represented, and advocated for me for over twenty-five years. Her wisdom, candour, and eternal good cheer have truly been a gift.

Doug Richmond, Janie Yoon, and Maria Golikova, my editors at House of Anansi Press, gave me endless encouragement, support, patience, and editorial wisdom which were essential to pulling my sprawling manuscript into its final form.

Sarah MacLachlan, president and publisher, and Matt Williams, vice president, at House of Anansi Press, brought me into their publishing "family" with my book *Is Work Killing You?* and allowed me to return with *Authenticity* and the chance to finally bring this book from idea to reality.

And lastly, my patients, who have shared their lives and stories with me for over thirty years. Their experiences, struggles, and victories are both an inspiration for others and what continues to fuel my passion for my work.

RESOURCES

Introduction

2   *Journalist Arianna Huffington tells the story*: Arianna Huffington, *The Sleep Revolution: Transforming Your Life, One Night at a Time* (New York: Harmony Books, 2016), 1–3.

Chapter 1

8   *a book about introversion*: Susan Cain, *Quiet: The Power of Introverts in a World That Can't Stop Talking* (New York: Crown Publishing, 2012), 13.

9   *Lesley Sword*: Lesley Sword, "Introversion-Extraversion Indicator," 2003, http://www.giftedservices.com.au/handouts/Introversion%20-%20 Extraversion%20Checklist.doc (accessed July 17, 2017).

Chapter 2

12   *I wrote away for his article*: Brian R. Little, MD, "Personality Myths about Leaders," *LEADERS*, 1989, 189–192.

14–15   *personality traits*: Brian R. Little, MD, *Me, Myself, and Us: The Science of Personality and the Art of Well-being* (Toronto: HarperCollins, 2014).

15   *"Why do extroverts have voice mail?"*: Devora Zack, *Networking for People Who Hate Networking: A Field Guide for Introverts, the Overwhelmed, and the Underconnected* (Oakland: Berrett-Koehler, 2010).

Chapter 3

19–20   *Marti Olsen Laney*: Marti Olsen Laney and Michael L. Laney, *The Introvert and Extrovert in Love: Making It Work When Opposites Attract* (Oakland: New Harbinger, 2007), 4.

21   *the "United Nations Dance"*: Quoted in Brian R. Little, MD, "Personality Myths about Leaders," *LEADERS*, 1989, 191.

22–23   *most of the talking*: Rebecca Knight, "How to Be Good at Managing Both Introverts and Extroverts," *Harvard Business Review*, November 16, 2015, https://hbr.org/2015/11/how-to-be-good-at-managing-both-introverts-and-extroverts (accessed June 22, 2017).

24   *Memory is organized differently*: Brian R. Little, MD, *Me, Myself, and Us: The Science of Personality and the Art of Well-being* (Toronto: HarperCollins, 2014), 40.

24–25   *short-term memory*: Brian R. Little, MD, "Personality Myths about Leaders," *LEADERS*, 1989, 190.

24   *open concept offices*: Susan Cain, *Quiet: The Power of Introverts in a World That Can't Stop Talking* (New York: Crown Publishing, 2012), 84.

27   *"It's easier to sedate an extravert than an introvert"*: Brian R. Little, MD, "Personality Myths about Leaders," *LEADERS*, 1989, 189.

Chapter 4

30   *levels of arousal*: Susan Cain, *Quiet: The Power of Introverts in a World That Can't Stop Talking* (New York: Crown Publishing, 2012), 158–162.

31–32   "fixed traits" and *"free traits"*: Brian R. Little, MD, *Me, Myself, and Us: The Science of Personality and the Art of Well-being* (Toronto: HarperCollins, 2014), 49–55.

33   *Angela Kasner*: Michael Petrou, "Angela Merkel: The real leader of the free world," *Maclean's*, February 20, 2015, http://www.macleans.ca/politics/angela-merkel-the-real-leader-of-the-free-world (accessed July 10, 2017).

Chapter 6

42   *A Q&A with Dr. Brian Little*: Brian Little, interview with the author.

Chapter 7

47   *"recovery rituals and routines"*: Jim Loehr and Tony Schwartz, *The Power of Full Engagement: Managing Energy, Not Time, Is the Key to High Performance and Personal Renewal* (New York: The Free Press, 2003), 32.

48–49   *Conversations between extraverts*: Rebecca Knight, "How to Be Good at Managing Both Introverts and Extroverts," *Harvard Business Review*, November 16, 2015, https://hbr.org/2015/11/how-to-be-good-at-managing-both-introverts-and-extroverts (accessed June 22, 2017).

Chapter 8

59   *Titles of books reflect this*: Brigid Schulte, *Overwhelmed: Work, Love, and Play When No One Has the Time* (New York: Harper Perennial, 2014); Thomas L. Friedman, *Thank You for Being Late: An Optimist's Guide to Thriving in the Age of Accelerations* (New York: Farrar, Straus and Giroux, 2016); Edward M. Hallowell, MD, *CrazyBusy: Overstretched, Overbooked, and About to Snap! Strategies for Handling Your Fast-Paced Life* (New York: Ballantine Books, 2007).

Chapter 9

62   *Compelling answers*: Jeremy Rifkin, *Time Wars: The Primary Conflict in Human History* (New York: Simon & Schuster, 1989).

62–63   *Annual migration of the swallows*: Ibid., 40.

64   *The "week" originated as the interval of time*: Ibid., 65.

64   *Computers refined the process*: Ibid., 23; Tracy Kidder, *The Soul of a New Machine* (New York: Little Brown, 1981), 137.

Chapter 10

66   *The purpose of time*: Jeremy Rifkin, *Time Wars: The Primary Conflict in Human History* (New York: Simon & Schuster, 1989), 94, 102, 123–141.

66–67   *Sir Sandford Fleming*: Clarke Blaise, *Time Lord: Sir Sandford Fleming and the Creation of Standard Time* (New York: First Vintage Books, 2000), 81–82.

71   *machinery dictated the tempo*: Jeremy Rifkin, *Time Wars: The Primary Conflict in Human History* (New York: Simon & Schuster, 1989), 105.

71   *"growth is good" and "more is better"*: Joe Dominguez and Vicki Robin, *Your Money or Your Life: 9 Steps to Transforming Your Relationship with Money and Achieving Financial Independence* (New York: Viking, 1992), 13.

71   *"more/faster/now"*: Vince Poscente, *The Age of Speed: Learning to Thrive in a More-Faster-Now World* (New York: Ballantine Books, 2008), 3.

Chapter 12

83–84   *A "sense of time urgency"*: Meyer Friedman, MD, and Ray H. Rosenman, MD, *Type A Behavior and Your Heart* (New York: Alfred A. Knopf, 1974), 4, 59, 231.

86   *an article in the* Canadian Medical Association Journal: Robert Buckman, MD, "A portrait of the doctor and his word processor," *CMAJ* 140 (June 1, 1989), 1361.

91   *"harnessing the power of speed"*: Vince Poscente, *The Age of Speed: Learning to Thrive in a More-Faster-Now World* (New York: Ballantine Books, 2008).

91–92   *"helps people spend less time"*: Ibid., 8.

93   *pendulum clocks*: Stephan Rechtschaffen, MD, *Time Shifting: Creating More Time to Enjoy Your Life* (New York: Doubleday, 1996), 22.

94   *music is the most effective entrainer*: Ibid., 25.

95   *a world that has speeded up dramatically*: Ibid., 26.

Chapter 14

104   *"Sleep is the single most effective thing"*: Quoted in Alice Park, "The Sleep Cure: The Fountain of Youth May Be Closer Than You Ever Thought," *Time*, February 15, 2017, http://time.com/4672988/the-sleep-cure-fountain-of-youth/ (accessed June 21, 2017).

105   *Dr. Stanley Coren*: Stanley Coren, interview with the author.

106   *Gallup poll*: Jeffrey M. Jones, "In U.S., 40% Get Less Than Recommended Amount of Sleep," *Gallup*, December 19, 2013, http://www.gallup.com/poll/166553/less-recommended-amount-sleep.aspx (accessed July 5, 2017).

106   *Statistics Canada*: Quoted in Joy D'Souza, "The True Cost of Sleep Deprivation is in the Billions," *Huffington Post*, November 30, 2016, http://www.huffingtonpost.ca/2016/11/30/cost-of-sleep-deprivation_n_13330508.html (accessed July 17, 2017).

106   *National Sleep Foundation poll*: National Sleep Foundation, "How much sleep do you get on weekdays?" (poll), http://www.drowsydriving.org (accessed July 17, 2017).

106–107   *"a study by Dr. Coren"*: Stanley Coren, *Sleep Thieves: An Eye-Opening Exploration into the Science and Mysteries of Sleep* (New York: The Free Press, 1996), 276.

107   *Ipsos-Reid study*: Ipsos Reid, "Many Canadians Feeling 'Free Time Crunch,'" March 8, 2001, https://www.ipsos.com/en-ca/many-canadians-feeling-free-time-crunch (accessed June 22, 2017).

107   *"The research about sleep deprivation"*: Charles Czeisler, MD, quoted in Karen Weintraub, "We Need More Sleep," *Boston Globe*, January 13, 2014, https://www.bostonglobe.com/lifestyle/

health-wellness/2014/01/13/sleep-more-important-than-you-might-think/1R6iiCYWbCSKY1K2wmwOVP/story.html (accessed July 5, 2017).

Chapter 15

109   *genetic mutation*: Hyun Hor and Mehdi Tafti, "How Much Sleep Do We Need?" *Science* 325, no. 5942 (August 14, 2009): 825–826; doi:10.1126/science.1178713.

109   *1 percent*: Arianna Huffington, *The Sleep Revolution: Transforming Your Life, One Night at a Time* (New York: Harmony Books, 2016), 117.

112   *"Body clocks reset themselves"*: Quoted in William C. Dement, MD, Ph.D., and Christopher Vaughan, *The Promise of Sleep: A Pioneer in Sleep Medicine Explains the Vital Connection Between Health, Happiness, and a Good Night's Sleep* (New York: Delacorte Press, 1999), 117.

Chapter 16

117   *point of IQ*: Stanley Coren, "Stolen Slumber," *Toronto Star*, February 7, 1999.

117   *sleep deprivation*: Ernest L. Rossi, Ph.D., with David Nimmons, *The 20 Minute Break* (New York: St. Martin's Press, 1991), 114.

117   *"Some pretty dumb things"*: Quoted in Stanley Coren, *Sleep Thieves: An Eye-Opening Exploration into the Science and Mysteries of Sleep* (New York: The Free Press, 1996), 78.

119   *Without adequate sleep, "you get sick, fat, and stupid"*: Russell Sanna, quoted in Karen Weintraub, "We Need More Sleep," *Boston Globe*, January 13, 2014, https://www.bostonglobe.com/lifestyle/health-wellness/2014/01/13/sleep-more-important-than-you-might-think/1R6iiCYWbCSKY1K2wmwOVP/story.html (accessed July 5, 2017).

120   *Statistics suggest that*: Arianna Huffington, *The Sleep Revolution: Transforming Your Life, One Night at a Time* (New York: Harmony Books, 2016), 32.

120   *another sobering piece of information*: Stanley Coren, "Stolen Slumber," *Toronto Star*, February 7, 1999.

Chapter 17

123   *electronic wristbands*: Ken Belson, "To the N.F.L., 40 Winks Is as Vital as the 40-Yard Dash," *New York Times*, October 1, 2016, https://www.nytimes.

com/2016/10/02/sports/football/nfl-players-sleep.html?mcubz=0 (accessed June 21, 2017).

124   *"power nap"*: James B. Maas, MD, *Power Sleep: The Revolutionary Program That Prepares Your Mind for Peak Performance* (New York: Villard Books, 1998), 106.

125   *napping at the job*: Camille and Bill Anthony, *The Art of Napping at Work* (New York: Larson Publications, 1999), 13.

126   *These minislumbers are called "microsleeps"*: James B. Maas, MD, *Power Sleep: The Revolutionary Program That Prepares Your Mind for Peak Performance* (New York: Villard Books, 1998), 49.

126   *drowsiness is not the first sign of impending sleep*: William C. Dement, MD, Ph.D., and Christopher Vaughan, *The Promise of Sleep: A Pioneer in Sleep Medicine Explains the Vital Connection Between Health, Happiness, and a Good Night's Sleep* (New York: Delacorte Press, 1999), 54.

127   *three interrelated factors affecting sleep*: Ibid., 127.

127   *melatonin actually rises*: Colin Shapiro, interview with the author.

131   *every night more than fifty million Americans stop breathing*: William C. Dement, MD, Ph.D., and Christopher Vaughan, *The Promise of Sleep: A Pioneer in Sleep Medicine Explains the Vital Connection Between Health, Happiness, and a Good Night's Sleep* (New York: Delacorte Press, 1999), 168.

131   *"In all of medicine"*: Ibid., 170.

132–133   *"We simply ask"*: Ibid., 139.

133   *RLS Foundation*: William C. Dement, MD, Ph.D., and Christopher Vaughan, *The Promise of Sleep: A Pioneer in Sleep Medicine Explains the Vital Connection Between Health, Happiness, and a Good Night's Sleep* (New York: Delacorte Press, 1999), 168.

Chapter 18

136   *As sleep expert Dr. James Maas says*: "Million Dollar Round Table Convention" (speech, Toronto, ON, 2008).

Chapter 19

151–152   *Baron Gottfried von Cramm*: Marshall Jon Fisher, *A Terrible Splendor: Three Extraordinary Men, a World Poised for War, and the Greatest Tennis Match Ever Played* (New York: Crown Publishers, 2009), 15.

153–154   *a recent CBC story*: Erica Johnson, "'I will do anything I can to make my goal': TD teller says customers pay price for 'unrealistic' sales targets," *CBC News*, March 6, 2017, http://www.cbc.ca/news/canada/british-columbia/td-tellers-desperate-to-meet-increasing-sales-goals-1.4006743 (accessed June 21, 2017).

155   *"our values are those principles and qualities that matter to us"*: Joe Dominguez and Vicki Robin, *Your Money or Your Life: 9 Steps to Transforming Your Relationship with Money and Achieving Financial Independence* (New York: Viking, 1992), 118–119.

Chapter 20

158   *The Ford Pinto*: Ben Wojdyla, "The Top Automotive Engineering Failures: The Ford Pinto Fuel Tanks," *Popular Mechanics*, May 20, 2011, http://www.popularmechanics.com/cars/a6700/top-automotive-engineering-failures-ford-pinto-fuel-tanks (accessed July 17, 2017).

159–160   *Lynden Dorval*: "Lynden Dorval, fired for giving zeros, 'treated unfairly,' appeal board rules," *CBC News*, August 29, 2014, http://www.cbc.ca/news/canada/edmonton/lynden-dorval-fired-for-giving-zeros-treated-unfairly-appeal-board-rules-1.2751007 (accessed June 21, 2017).

161   *"referability habits"*: Dan Sullivan, *How the Best Get Better: The Art and Science of Entrepreneurial Success* (Toronto: Strategic Coach, 2001), 30.

164–165   *outbreak of Listeria*: "How Maple Leaf Foods is handling the Listeria outbreak," *CBC News*, August 28, 2008, http://www.cbc.ca/news/business/how-maple-leaf-foods-is-handling-the-listeria-outbreak-1.763404 (accessed June 21, 2017).

Chapter 21

177   *Dan Price*: Patricia Cohen, "One Company's New Minimum Wage: $70,000 a Year," *New York Times*, April 13, 2015, https://www.nytimes.com/2015/04/14/business/owner-of-gravity-payments-a-credit-card-processor-is-setting-a-new-minimum-wage-70000-a-year.html?mcubz=0 (accessed June 21, 2017).

177   *CNN reported*: Charles Riley and Poppy Harlow, "Gravity Payments CEO defends $70,000 minimum salary," *CNN*, August 10, 2015, http://money.cnn.com/2015/08/09/news/gravity-payments-dan-price-70k-salary/index.html (accessed June 22, 2017).

178–179   *The emphasis on money and fund-raising*: Ryan Grim and Sabrina Siddiqui, "Call Time For Congress Shows How Fundraising Dominates Bleak Work Life," Huffington Post, January 8, 2013, http://www.huffingtonpost.ca/

entry/call-time-congressional-fundraising_n_2427291 (accessed July 10, 2017).

179–180   *In her book*: Marlo Thomas, *The Right Words at the Right Time* (New York: Simon & Schuster, 2002), 125.

180   *"resumé virtues" and "eulogy virtues"*: David Brooks, *The Road to Character* (New York: Random House, 2015), xi.

180   *"the culture of the Big Me"*: Ibid., 6.

Chapter 22

181   *Jean Béliveau*: Tu Thanh Ha, "Four great moves that testify to Jean Béliveau's class off the ice," *Globe and Mail*, December 3, 2014, https://www.theglobeandmail.com/sports/hockey/beliveau-remembered-for-class-generosity-off-the-ice/article21905226/ (accessed June 21, 2017).

187   *Roger Mellott's wise saying*: Roger Mellott, *Stress Management for Professionals: How to Feel Better and Perform Better on the Job* (Colorado: CareerTrack Publications, 1987). Audiobook.

189   *Robin Sharma's inspirational megabestseller*: Robin Sharma, *The Monk Who Sold His Ferrari: A Fable About Fulfilling Your Dreams and Reaching Your Destiny* (New York: HarperCollins, 1998).

Chapter 23

191   *do more of what works and less of what doesn't*: Michele Weiner-Davis, *Change Your Life and Everyone in It* (New York: Simon & Schuster, 1995), 19.

Chapter 25

214   *we don't have a clear understanding of ourselves*: Peter Caven, "A practical alternative to 'following your passion,'" *Globe and Mail*, March 1, 2017, https://www.theglobeandmail.com/report-on-business/careers/leadership-lab/smarter-alternative-advice-to-merely-following-your-passion/article34109902/ (accessed June 21, 2017).

Chapter 26

219   *"take a few moments now to reflect upon your dreams"*: Joe Dominguez and Vicki Robin, *Your Money or Your Life: 9 Steps to Transforming Your*

Relationship with Money and Achieving Financial Independence (New York: Viking, 1992), 109.

221–222   *Kris's Story*: CBC Radio interview, February 4, 2010.

223–224   *Alex's Story*: Richard Griffin, "'Kid' Alex Anthopoulos takes over as Jays GM," *Toronto Star*, October 4, 2009, https://www.thestar.com/opinion/2009/10/04/kid_alex_anthopoulos_takes_over_as_jays_gm.html (accessed June 21, 2017); Bruce Arthur, "Blue Jays a labour of love for GM Alex Anthopoulos," *Toronto Star*, October 3, 2015, https://www.thestar.com/sports/baseball/2015/10/04/blue-jays-a-labour-of-love-for-gm-alex-anthopoulos-arthur.html (accessed June 21, 2017).

224   *"I forgot that having fun is an option"*: Michael Held, interview with the author.

Chapter 29

244   *allowing your "calling" to come to you*: Ryan Holmes, "When You Shouldn't Follow Your Heart," *Entrepreneur*, May 14, 2015, https://www.entrepreneur.com/article/246212 (accessed June 21, 2017).

244   *"follow your passion"*: Cal Newport, "Follow a Career Passion? Let It Follow You," *New York Times*, September 29, 2012, http://www.nytimes.com/2012/09/30/jobs/follow-a-career-passion-let-it-follow-you.html?mcubz=0 (accessed June 21, 2017).

246   *One particular book I love*: David McCullough, *Truman* (New York: Simon & Schuster, 1992).

248–249   *In his excellent TED book*: Barry Schwartz, *Why We Work* (New York: Simon & Schuster, 2015), 15.

INDEX

To contact Dr. Posen for speaking engagements or seminars,
please call or write:

David B. Posen, MD
1235 Trafalgar Road
Suite 406
Oakville, Ontario
Canada L6H 3P1

Telephone: (905) 844-0744
Toll-free: 1-800-806-2307
Email: david@davidposen.com
www.davidposen.com